Prophet in Exile

Studies in Modern European History

Frank J. Coppa
General Editor

Vol. 3

PETER LANG
New York • Bern • Frankfurt am Main • Paris

William Roberts

Prophet in Exile

Joseph Mazzini in England, 1837-1868

PETER LANG
New York • Bern • Frankfurt am Main • Paris

Library of Congress Cataloging-in-Publication Data

Roberts, William
  Prophet in exile.
  (Studies in modern European history ; vol. 3)
  Bibliography: p.
1. Mazzini, Giuseppe, 1805-1872.   2. Italy—Politics and
government—1815-1870.   3. Great Britain—Intellectual
life—19th century.   4. Revolutionists—Italy—Biography.
5. Statesmen—Italy—Biography.   I. Title.   II. Series.
DG552.8.M3R67   1989   945'.08'092 [B]   89-2706
ISBN 0-8204-1051-9
ISSN 0893-6897

CIP-Titelaufnahme der Deutschen Bibliothek

Roberts, William:
Prophet in exile : Joseph Mazzini in England,
1837–1868 / William Roberts. New York; Bern;
Frankfurt am Main; Paris: Lang, 1989.
  (Studies in Modern European History; Vol. 3)
  ISBN 0-8204-1051-9

NE: GT

Printed by Weihert-Druck GmbH, Darmstadt, West Germany

To My Family

Giuseppe Mazzini

PREFACE

The Italian nationalist Joseph Mazzini (1805-1872) spent more than half of his adult life as an exile in England. During his periods of exile (1837-1848, 1850-1859, 1861-1868) he was in contact with the major figures of the age, both British and foreign. They included John Stuart Mill, Thomas Carlyle, such Chartists and radicals as William J. Linton, George Jacob Holyoake, Joseph Cowen, and William Lovett, and also leading continental exiles residing in London, including Karl Marx, Alexander Herzen, Louis Kossuth, and Stanislaus Worcell. The purpose of this work is to investigate the relationship between Mazzini and some of these important figures, and to compare their respective philosophies, ideas, and political programs.

Because of Mazzini's long years in England, his numerous associations with leading intellectuals and radicals, and his place in the history of ideas, particular questions arise which will also be addressed. What effect did the exile have on his revolutionary zeal -- was it tempered or enhanced, especially as he observed the course of politics in Great Britain? Did the English and foreign thinkers with whom he associated have a specific influence on his positivist philosophy and his revolutionary program for Italy and the rest of Europe? The ideas of liberty, morality, duty, and religion appear constantly in his writings. How do they compare with or differ from those of Mill or Marx, Carlyle or Holyoake? Mazzini began his career as a decided nationalist and ended it as an internationalist. What effect did the exile have on this aspect of his thought? What part did the exile play in his becoming perhaps more of a social than a nationalistic writer? And what was his relationship with the other Italians, both of the. middle and working classes, who had also settled in London? One of the difficulties in writing about Mazzini is the need to integrate an extremely active political career with that of a most prolific writer and thinker. There was not a time of more than a few months when Mazzini was politically inactive or only writing and speculating.

An important underlying question concerns the extent to which Mazzini served as a conduit for various systems of British and continental thought and the extent to which he synthesized these systems. Mazzini seems to represent several distinct modes of western thought. Elements of his writings on duty and morality echo Kant. Yet his views of a positivistic society are reminiscent of St. Simon and Comte, although he himself was critical of these thinkers. Mazzini's view of history is teleologic and deterministic, especially concerning the role nations and peoples, each ordained by Providence for a specific role in the unfolding of human progress. It is the identification of this particular role or "mission" which defines Mazzini's proposed Italian state; here the Hegelian or Coleridgian strain is evident.

Mazzini's writings on charity and public relief in Great Britain recall Tocqueville's essay on the subject. "Millions of pounds," Mazzini wrote in 1844, "are spent annually here in England for the relief of individuals who have fallen into want; ... yet want increases here every year."(1) What effect did such observations have on Mazzini's own economic theories, which were strongly critical of both British utilitarianism and European socialism? Mazzini seems to incorporate or amalgamate diverse views. Did this process continue in the last years of his life, when new systems of thought, were emerging, and, did they in turn, serve to modify his concepts of democracy, nationalism, and internationalism?

Finally, Mazzini is portrayed by most of his biographers as single-minded and unchanging, not only in his thought but also in his policy. Indeed, he complimented the English on their "tenacity and harmony of thought and action."(2) But did he actually remain as steadfast and unchanging in his own policy and philosophy during the long exile as some historians suggest?

These questions provide a new perspective on the development of radical thought in the nineteenth century. As Mazzini was both a central figure in the history of modern nationalism, as well as a channel for diverse currents of opinion and policy, an analysis of his long period of exile in England -- the nation he came to regard as his "real home"(3) -- will contribute to a better understanding of Mazzini and his role in the development of nineteenth century radical and nationalistic thought.

Notes

(1) Joseph Mazzini, The Life and Writings of Joseph Mazzini (6 vols., London, 1898), 4:48 ("The Duties of Man," 1844).

(2) Ibid., p. 67.

(3) Giuseppe Mazzini, *Scritti editi ed inediti*, ed. A. Codignola, G. Daelli, E. Morelli, V. E. Orlando, et. al. (98 vols., Imola, 1905-1973), 81:167 (letter to E. Venturi, May 1867).

ACKNOWLEDGMENTS

This work developed out of a lifelong interest in the writings and work of Mazzini. While not pretending to be a definitive biography -- an enterprise which would require not one but several volumes, this present study focuses on a most significant and productive period of his life -- his British exile.

During the course of the research and writing of this project I have incurred many debts. First, I want to acknowledge my family -- my parents Elizabeth and William Roberts, and my sister Elizabeth -- for their consistent and invaluable encouragement, for their patience, and for their support in this endeavor.

Among friends, historians, and mentors I would like to thank Gertrude Himmelfarb of the City University of New York for her guidance and advice during research and writing and for providing the intellectual stimulation which in part inspired this effort. Likewise, I am grateful to Frank J. Coppa, of St. John's University, for being a source of encouragement and assistance and especially for his unwavering confidence in my work. I want also to express my appreciation to Joel H. Wiener of City University, who read my manuscript and offered advice and suggestions, especially regarding the section on Chartism.

A special thanks is due to the librarians of Fairleigh Dickinson University and the City University of New York, especially the reference departments for their kind help, as well as the production staff at Peter Lang for their assistance. Finally, I want to thank all my friends, colleagues, and students for their moral support and encouragement.

TABLE OF CONTENTS

CHAPTER I

INTRODUCTION

Joseph Mazzini was born in Genoa, Italy, in 1805. He was the only son of Dr. Giovanni Mazzini, a physician, and Maria Drago, a woman of strong Jansenist beliefs. Both parents had been inspired by the principles of the French Revolution, and Jacobin texts and pamphlets were always in the home. Discussions with Italian liberals and nationalists were frequent in Mazzini's childhood. In 1800, Dr. Mazzini briefly held a minor position in the newly created Bonapartist Ligurian Republic and the absorption in 1821 of that state by the Kingdom of Piedmont would be a source of bitter resentment to the republican Mazzini family.(1)

In his memoirs in 1864 Mazzini also recalled 1821 as the year of his own political awakening:

> One Sunday in April, 1821, while I was yet a boy I was walking in the Strada Nuova with my mother and an old friend ... The Piedmontese insurrection had just been crushed; partly by Austria, partly through treachery, and partly through the weakness of its leaders.

> The revolutionists, seeking safety by sea, had flocked to Genoa ... they went about seeking help to enable them to cross into Spain, where the revolution was yet triumphant and I used to search them out from amongst our own people, detecting them either by their general appearance ... or by the signs of a deep and silent sorrow on their faces.

> Presently we were stopped and addressed by a tall black-bearded man with a severe and energetic countenance ... I have never since forgotten. He held out a white handkerchief ... merely saying, "for the refugees of Italy." My mother and a friend dropped some money into the handkerchief...

That day was the first in which a confused idea presented itself to my mind -- I will not say of country or of liberty -- but an idea that we Italians 'could' and therefore 'ought' to struggle for the liberty of our country.(2)

Mazzini at this time was a student at the University of Genoa, where he continued to read works of the French and German Enlightenment and dream of Italian unification. He also made the friendship of the Ruffini family, whose two sons, Agostino and Giovanni, were later to join him in his first English exile. Mazzini developed a following among the students at the University, and as a somber romantic clad in black, was a natural leader. By 1825, there were already police references to Mazzini and his "Mazzinians."

It was also at this time that he began to write, and one of his works, an essay on Walter Scott in the *Indicatore Genovese*, caused that small newspaper to be investigated by the police. The strong censorship of the period equated enthusiastic romanticism with political extremism. In 1826, Mazzini submitted an article, "Dante's Love of Country," to the *Antologia*, the best Italian literary review of the time. The subject is significant since Mazzini represented Dante as one of the earliest advocates of Italian unity; and although the article was at first rejected, it was later printed in that journal.(3)

In 1827 two important events occurred in Mazzini's life. He graduated as Doctor of Law and, with Jacopo Ruffini, joined the Carbonari. The origins of the Carbonari, or "Charcoal Burners," are obscure, since it used the death penalty to protect its secrets. During the Napoleonic period it was strong in Murat's Kingdom of Naples as a secret anti-Bonapartist movement and subsequently spread throughout Italy, taking on the aspects of Freemasonry, including networks of secret lodges and extreme anticlericalism and anti-papalism; it was the Carbonari who directed the unsuccessful revolutions in Naples and Turin in 1820 and 1821. Its headquarters, the "Central Lodge," or *Venditta*, was at Berne, Switzerland until 1830 when it moved to Paris. The organization's main plan until 1830 had been to attack the restoration settlement in Spain, but after July 1830, it focused again on Italy, with the national headquarters located at Genoa.(4) It was hoped that the July Revolution in France would inspire similar risings throughout the Italian states.

Mazzini had joined the Carbonari at the suggestion of a fellow law student, Pietro Torre, who offered to initiate him into the order. Mazzini accepted, but afterward confessed his disappointment that in the initiation ceremony nothing was said explicitly about Italian unity or federalism. "I reflected with surprise that the oath administered to me was a mere formula of obedience."(5) He asked Torre for more information, but Torre declined, only congratulating him for having undergone a brief and mild form of initiation. Characteristically, Mazzini threw himself into the movement. An "Apprentice" in 1827, he was by 1829 a "Master" and Secretary of the Genoa branch of the order. As Secretary, he wrote a pamphlet in French, *Spain In 1829, Considered in Relation to France*, addressed to Charles X. In the same year he addressed a letter in faltering English to the Irish nationalist Daniel 0 'Connell(6) There is from this period an early account of Mazzini which shows the extent to which his Romantic personality and mien attracted his contemporaries. Mazzini was described by one compatriot as being dressed all in black (a style that he affected most of his life), with a large "republican" hat, having a "noble" brow and a countenance through which shown "a power of firmness and decision" that mingled with the "gaiety and sweetness" of his eyes.(7) A police circular of the time confirmed this view, and added that Mazzini also had an "attractive, sonorous voice," was a "ready speaker" of "noble carriage," and was "energetic in all his actions."(8)

The July Revolution in France convinced the Carbonari that an Italian revolution was imminent and Mazzini traveled south to Tuscany to organize the branch there. During his absence, the existence of the Genoa branch was betrayed to the police. On his return in November, Mazzini was arrested and imprisoned for three months in the sea-front fortress of Savona. Although Mazzini was isolated from the other prisoners, his imprisonment was not extremely harsh. He had his books -- the Bible, Tacitus, and Byron -- letters from his family, and visitors, including the governor of the prison and his wife who would sometimes visit for after-dinner coffee. Through codes with fellow prisoners Mazzini learned of outside events, including the Polish uprising of 1831.(9) As a result of the Carbonari's failures in a series of attempted risings in central Italy and its lack of a populist program, Mazzini at this time became disillusioned with the organization.

In February 1831 a government commission ruled that, although the existence of a Carbonaro lodge at Genoa could not be proved, the prisoners already taken would be given the choice of rural retirement or foreign exile. Mazzini chose exile. With his uncle he traveled first to Geneva, then Lyons, always meeting and conspiring with Italian exiles along the way. French police harassment drove them finally to Marseilles, where Mazzini came under the influence of the St. Simonians. In Marseilles, Mazzini set to work founding his Federation of Young Italy. It was to be the basis for his subsequent republican plans for Italy and for the broader scheme of a Young Europe movement. Mazzini incorporated element of Kantian morality, into this movement. "There is a law of Kant, that defines, admirably, the moral mission of European youth: act as if each of your actions were to become a Universal law."(10) Young Italy soon replaced the Carbonari, on which it was closely modeled, as the new hope of the Italian liberal movement with Mazzini's charismatic personality proving essential to the organization's growth.

In June 1832, Mazzini's writings and activities among the Italian exiles provoked the French authorities who ordered him out of the country. He went to Geneva where he was strategically in a better position to lead an expedition into Italy which was supposed to signal a general rising against the Piedmontese monarchy. While in Geneva, Mazzini founded Young Europe and led the expedition known as the Second Savoy Raid, which included that organization's German, Polish, and Spanish delegates. The First Savoy Raid, an expedition into Italy, had been attempted in March 1831. That plan involved the capture of Savoy and the establishment of a republic in that province, and, it was hoped would produce subsequent risings in Piedmont, Liguria, and throughout the rest of Italy. The First Savoy Raid failed, but Mazzini and his disciples hoped that a second expedition would succeed and that the Italian revolution would become the model for European-wide revolts.

From its inception, the second Savoy expedition had problems. Quarrels over the military command of the company, harassment by the Swiss authorities, and the capture of some of the members of the German and Polish contingents delayed the transalpine campaign until the winter months. With Mazzini ill, the expedition became completely demoralized and it failed.

Mazzini, now in hiding in Switzerland, faced this crisis with renewed hope and activity. He prepared, for example, a Young Switzerland pamphlet in which he advocated a stronger federal government and an explicitly anti-Austrian foreign policy for Switzerland.(11) It was also at this time that he came strongly under the influence of the French liberal Catholic thinker Felicite-Robert Lamennais. In the notebooks he had kept as a university student, he had included Lamennais' "Essay on Indifference," published in 1817, among the works that he believed should be used to stimulate literary studies in Italy.(12) And in 1834, during has Swiss exile, he wrote: "Lamennais *Words of A Believer* has stupified me! There is true power in that book as in all of his."(13) Mazzini would eventually meet Lamennais, and introduced him to several of the British Chartists when they accompanied him to Paris in 1848.

What attracted Mazzini to Lamennais was his theology. Lamennais had amalgamated the ideas of such thinkers as Rousseau with Catholic doctrine replacing, for example, the authority of the Catholic hierarchy with that of the "People" or the "General Wall." He had also separated the St. Simonian concepts of Progress, Humanity and Association from their materialistic connotations. This fit perfectly into Mazzini's developing political philosophy, in which he was attempting to deal with the utilitarian element that he found in French positivism.

Expelled by the Swiss and subsequently the French authorities Mazzini, came to England in January 1837, several months before Victoria began her reign. With him were the Ruffini brothers and a fellow-nationalist Angelo Usiglio. About this time, a rumor circulated in Genoa that Mazzini had been appointed Lord Palmerston's secretary. Nothing was further from the truth. Four years earlier, Camillo Cavour, the future prime minister of Piedmont and Mazzini's lifelong antagonist, had visited London with letters of introduction admitting him to the best circles. He met with Tocqueville, heard Peel speak in Commons, and addressed the Royal Geographical Society. Cavour returned to Italy with plans for railroads and steamships for Piedmont and Genoa. By contrast, Mazzini, and his three companions, slipped into London unnoticed, passing from the Hotel Sablonniere to modest lodgings at 24 Goodge Street, Tottenham Court Road. His father and a family friend had provided him with a letter of introduction to Italians in London, but since none of these were republicans Mazzini refused to deal with them.

Life in England began for Mazzini in what he later called a "crisis of absolute poverty."(14) The cost of living was so high that he could rarely afford even small luxuries. His father advised him to teach Italian, but Mazzini replied that there were already too many language teachers and anyway the idea was boring.(15) Instead, he preferred to make his living by writing. Meanwhile the exiles survived on meager supplements from the Ruffini and Mazzini families.

The nature of the city was also at first discouraging to Mazzini. "In this sunless and musicless land," he wrote, "we have lost even the sky, which the veriest wretch on the continent can look at."(16) One thing that did appeal to him was the fog. "When you look up, the eye loses itself in a reddish, bell-shaped vault, which always gives me, I don't know why, an idea of the phosphorescent light of the Inferno. The whole city seems under a kind of spell."(17) By August of the first year, he was writing to an Italian friend in Edinburgh that he might have to seek manual work, and letters to his mother told of exiled Polish officers whose poverty forced them to work on British railways.(18)

In November 1837 Mazzini was introduced to John Stuart Mill by a merchant John Taylor. Taylor's wife Harriet (who would eventually marry Mill) persuaded Mill to take Mazzini on as a writer for his journal, the *London and Westminster Review*.(19) The following month Mazzini wrote to his family, "The other day I met a certain Mill. He is the editor of a Radical review, and he asked me for articles, especially on the political situation in Italy."(20) In 1838 Mazzini met Thomas and Jane Welsh Carlyle who were to become his first English friends. To Jane, Mazzini would become a confidant, especially during a period of difficulty in her marriage. Of Carlyle himself, Mazzini's biographer Bolton King wrote that Mazzini "respected his sincerity, his freedom from insular narrowness, his outspokeness."(21) In 1843 Mazzini would present his opinion of Carlyle in his article "On the Genius and Tendency in the Writings of Thomas Carlyle" and in a review of Carlyle's *History of the French Revolution.*

During the first period of exile, 1837-1848, Mazzini made his living writing for the *London and Westminster Review, The Monthly Chronicle, The British and Foreign Review, Tait's Edinburgh Magazene,* and the radical *People's Journal.* But by 1841, some of these journals had closed down or stopped paying a pound a page and Mazzini had to find other means of making a living. In 1842, a Bolognese archaeologist proposed to ship to England a consignment of antiques. Mazzini was to receive and distribute the consignment and share in the profits. This added income would, if sufficient, free his time for propagandistic activities. Although the consignment arrived, the investment came to naught, and Mazzini had to fall back on loans from family, friends and London loansharks to stay solvent.(22)

In London Mazzini had his first real contact with the laboring classes and the poor, especially the poor Italian workers of the city. Among these were peasant children brought over from Italy under contracts that promised high pay but had no validity in England. The youths were exploited by their bosses, the worst of whom Mazzini finally succeeded in bringing to justice. But Mazzini wished to do something more for the victims. In November, 1841, he opened a school where the children and workers could come in the evening to learn reading and writing, and on Sundays, drawing and Italian history. Mazzini himself was a principal instructor and sympathizers rallied to his side, including Mill, Gabriele Rossetti, Mazzini's physician Joseph Toynbee, and the

Chartist William J. Linton. Mazzini also had political motives for establishing the school.

> The School ... afforded me a means of contact with the Italian workmen of London. I selected the best among them to help me in a work more directly national in its purpose. We formed an association of working-men, and published a journal called the *Apostolato Popolare*, bearing as a motto the words: 'Work and its proportionate recompense.'(23)

In 1841 Mazzini founded his "Working Men's Association" as a section of "Young Italy," and a central chapter of his *Duties of Man*, entitled "To the Italian Working Men," first appeared in the *Apostolato Popolare*. At the same time Mazzini began his involvement with British radicals, republicans, and Chartists - The first of these was Linton, through whom Mazzini met the freethinker George Jacob Holyoake, and other Chartists and radicals including William Lovett, George Julian Harney, Ernest Jones, and Joseph Cowen.

When the Ruffinis left London in 1841, Mazzini came to depend on his English friendships, moving within two overlapping circles, that of the working class radicals and that of the middle classes. Of the latter group, his closest friends, even more than the Carlyles, were the Ashursts of Muswell Hill -- "the clan," as they came to be called in Mazzini's letters -- "a dear, good, holy family, who surrounded me with such loving care, as sometimes to make me forget I was an exile."(24) William H. Ashurst was a solicitor who met Mazzini through the socialist thinker Robert Owen. One of the Ashurst daughters married Mazzini's friend James Stansfeld, and another Emilie, who became one of Mazzini's earliest biographers, married his compatriot Carlo Venturi. Still another daughter introduced him to George Sand.

Through both the Carlyles and the Ashursts Mazzini's circle of friends and acquaintances grew. Among Italians he met Gabriel Rossetti and his son Dante, and Antonio Panizzi, a leading supporter of Cavour and chief librarian at the British Museum. Among the English were Charles Dickens, who made a donation to the school, David Masson, biographer of Milton, and Benjamin Hawkes, Member of Parliament for Lambeth and later Secretary of State for the colonies.(25) He also met John Bowring, backer of the anti-Corn Law League and editor of the works of Bentham, the author Margaret Fuller, the poets Thomas Campbell and Samuel Rogers, and the American journalist Amos Alcott.(26)

Mazzini also became greatly involved at this time with fellow political exiles. The best known of these was the Polish republican, Stanislaus Worcell, who had taken part in the illfated Savoy expedition of 1832.(27) This Polish nobleman was also a mathematician, linguist, and philosopher and Mazzini frequently sought his company. Five years older than Mazzini, Worcell suffered from privation and illness, giving all his free time to revolutionary activity. Mazzini called him "a man to revere and love, a saintly martyr, a true hero," and to Mazzini Worcell confided has image of Poland as the suffering "Messiah-nation" that was to bring about the redemption of Europe.(28) Alexander Herzen more cynically described Worcell as believing "in a spiritual world, undefined, unnecessary, and impossible," and as following "the religion of George Sand, of Pierre Leroux, and Mazzini. (29) With Mazzini, Worcell was the leading political exile in London until the arrival of the refugees after the revolutions of 1878. However, as Worcell's health declined after 1841, Mazzini became even more the leading foreign revolutionary figure in England

In 1844, an event occurred which underscored this fact and brought Mazzini and his ideas to national attention. It was the revelation that the British postal authorities were opening Mazzini's mail and reporting the contents to the Austrian government. Mazzini had been writing about what was called the "Scheme of 1844" -- a series of "spontaneous" risings which lie had planned to occur in Italy against the ruling foreign powers. Revolutionaries put themselves at Mazzini's disposal, including two young Venetian nobles, Attilio and Emilio Bandiera, whose father was an admiral in the Austrian navy. At this time Mazzini became suspicious that the British Post Office was tampering with his correspondence. With the help of Linton, Lovett, and another Chartist, Henry Hetherington, Mazzini experimented with further letters containing grains of sand, and this, with a close examination of the seals on letters that he received from abroad, confirmed his suspicions.(30) Mazzini put the matter in the hands of Thomas Duncombe, Member of Parliament for Finsbury, and a storm of indignation followed the disclosure in the House of Commons. The Home Secretary, Sir James Graham, after initially denying the allegations, took the position that tampering with private correspondence was justified in cases of conspiracy.(31) Furthermore, he testified; he had never even heard of Mazzini until 1843, when the Austrian government had informed him that a dangerous revolutionary was in London. In January 1844 Lord Aberdeen, the Foreign Secretary, had reported that London was a center of revolutionary activity threatening European peace. Graham made further inquiries and was persuaded that Mazzini was "a dangerous adventurer whose movements should be closely observed."(32) As for the Bandieras, who after disregarding Mazzini's warnings, took part in an invasion of Italy and were seized and executed at Naples, Graham felt that they were the victims of "nothing but their extravagant passions and imprudence ... they rushed headlong to their own destruction."(33)

But public opinion was with Mazzini who saw the controversy as an opportunity to bring himself to national attention. Leading British figures, such as Dickens, Carlyle, Thomas Macaulay, and the Liberal M.P. R. Monckton Milnes took up the debate on Mazini's behalf - So did the press -- *Punch* published a series of satirical prints, showing "anti-Graham wafers," necessary for sealing and "maintaining the privacy of the mails."(34) The *Globe* published a letter from the leading Italians in England, thanking Duncombe and reaffirming their faith in Mazzini.(35) Panizzi wrote an article supporting Mazzini in the *North British Review*, and another in the *Westminster Review* entitled "The Morality of Politics," in which he traced the flaws in the government's argument against Mazzini and criticized its labeling of him as a conspirator and revolutionary without scruples or principles.(36) Carlyle's opinion of what came to be known as the "Post Office Scandal" was contained in has June 1844 letter to the *Times*:

> I have had the honor to know M. Mazzini for a series of years; and whatever I may thin] of his practical insight and skill in worldly affairs, I can testify that he ... is a man of genius and virtue, a man of sterling veracity, humanity, and nobleness of mind...

> Of Italian democracies and Young Italy's sorrows, of extraneous Austrian emperors in Milan or poor old chimerical popes in Bologna, I know nothing...But it is a question vital to us that sealed letters in an English post-office be, as we all fancied they were, respected as things sacred; that opening of men's letters, a practice near of kin to picking men's pockets ... be not resorted to except in cases of very last resort.(37)

The "Post Office Scandal" made Mazzini the best known political exile in England. This was as lie intended. In has autobiographical notes he wrote, "The incident of that violation afforded me an opportunity of bringing the hitherto neglected cause of my country before the eyes of England."(38) After the Post Office incident more support came for the Italian school and Mazzini undertook the rebuilding of Young Italy as the Italian National Association.

It had a broader basis than Young Italy, which had suffered setbacks in 1844, and Mazzini hoped that the new organization would have a wider appeal among British supporters. In 1847, he also formed the People's International League. It was the first popular association founded in Great Britain with the primary goal of influencing foreign policy. The Address of the Council of the People's International League described its objectives:

> to enlighten the British Public as to the political condition and relations of Foreign Countries, to disseminate the principles on national freedom and progress, to ... manifest an efficient public opinion in favour of the right of every People to self-government ... and to promote a good understanding between the Peoples of all nations.(39)

In the same year a rival organization, the Fraternal Democrats, had also been founded and it competed with the League for the loyalty of the revolutionary exiles in Great Britain. Mazzini and the League were more successful among the Italians and Poles while the Democrats attracted more Germans, many of whom were already socialists. In 1847 Harney and Jones, the militant Chartist leaders of the Democrats, made overtures to Marx and Engels, appealing to them in terms of a coming class war. Events on the continent would soon underscore the rivalry between the two organizations.

In the Fall of 1847 Mazzini visited Paris where he met with Lammenais and George Sand and became aware that revolution in Europe was eminent. When news of the formation of a Provisional government in Paris reached Mazzini and the League in February 1848, they decided to send a delegation to meet with the government's revolutionary leaders. In Paris, Mazzini introduced Linton to Lammenais and, following Mazzini's lead, the Fraternal Democrats sent a delegation led by Harney and Jones who also took this opportunity to meet with Marx and Engels.(40)

News of revolution in Italy reached Mazzini just as he arrived back in London. He hurried to Milan in time to participate in the "Five Days" April uprising against Austria. The "Five Days" marked the beginning of a series of uprisings throughout the country against the ducal and papal governments. Mazzini served with Garibaldi's volunteer army, which fought under a flag bearing the motto "God and the People," until November when the pope, Pius IX, fled from Rome and a republic was proclaimed with Mazzini as the leader of its ruling Triumvirate. In his first address to the Republic's Assembly Mazzini prophesied that the Rome of the emperors and of the popes would be followed by a third Rome, the Rome of the People.(41) He then sought to put into practice the ideals that he had for so long preached in exile.

In governing the republic Mazzini demonstrated toleration toward the Church and the papal establishment left in Rome. Confessionals which had been taken and used as barricades were ordered restored to the churches of the city, and Mazzini's one act of severity towards the clergy seems to have been the fine he imposed on the canons of St. Peter's for refusing to celebrate the usual Easter services. The nationalization of Church land was, however, proposed along with a program of broad agrarian reform. A defense force was formed under the leadership of Garibaldi and the direction of the Triumvirate.(42)

The pope, in exile near Naples, had hoped for an Austrian army to retake Rome and restore the papal government. Instead, help came from an unexpected source. The French, fearful of an Austrian force massing in Italy, ordered their army to attack Rome. After a month of fighting the city fell and, in July 1849, Mazzini and the other republican leaders fled into exile.

Mazzini, in hiding in Switzerland, wrote a reply to the French government's act ion which was published by the Italian Refugee Fund Committee in London. The pamphlet, "A Letter to Messrs. De Tocqueville and De Falloux, Ministers of France," was an attempt to refute the French claim that their armies had liberated Rome and saved it from anarchy. Mazzini argued that the Roman Republican government had been popularly elected, the Assembly itself consisting almost entirely of Roman citizens. The pope had already fled the city and it was the republicans who had saved Rome from anarchy. Finally, the French were castigated for having betrayed both their own republican ideals and their promises to the Roman Assembly that they would act only as protectors of the Republic.(43) Still hopeful of the possibility of revolution, Mazzini made a brief visit to Paris in the Spring of 1850 but soon realized that it would be futile to try to stop the rise of Louis Napoleon at that time. After a short visit to London, he then returned to Switzerland. In February 1851 he arrived again in London, where he was to make has home, with few interruptions, until the last years of his life. "Italy is my country, but England is my real home if I have any."(44) It was the beginning of his second period of exile, 1851-1858. His biographer, H. W. Rudman has noted the "astonishing degree" to which "Mazzini had intimately associated himself with English life and thought."(45) In a long letter to a follower Francesco Crispi, who was eager to learn about British life, Mazzini told him to read the *Westminster Review*; the *North British Review*, and the

Athenaeum to find out what was vital in contemporary English thinking. He also advised him to study Carlyle's works, since Carlyle was the antagonist of "democracy and of aristocracy at the same time, and "was the head of an important school which adored both the individual (or the hero) and fact, force, and success." Crispi, who would later become prime minister of Italy, was also advised to acquaint himself with the works of Mill, Tennyson, and the Brownings. "All other poets," Mazzini pronounced, "are mediocre." In religious thought Mazzini recommended Charles Kingsley and Francis Newman, in art Landseer, Ruskin, and the pre-Raphaelites.(46)

Mazzini's second period of exile was a time of change in England as well as in his own intellectual and political development. The new prosperity in England, marked by the Great Exposition of 1851 played a part in the evolution of Mazzini's views on domestic and foreign issues, including the question of non-intervention. The 1850's also brought another group of political refugees to England, including Marx, Herzen, Louis Blanc, Louis Kossuth, and Alexander Ledru-Rollin. All were to have an effect on Mazzini's ideas and work.

During this decade Mazzini was involved in the formation of various groups for the purposes of Italian unification and international revolution. These groups included the Italian Refugee Fund Committee, the Friends of Italy Society, and the Central Committee of European Democracy; the Central Committee was founded with Ledru-Rollin and Arnold Ruge and was a forerunner of the First International. Mazzini also renewed his involvement with the British radicals and Chartists. It was in response to Mazzini's first open profession of republicanism in England, in the essay, "Royalty and Republicanism in Italy," that Linton founded his journal, the *English Republic* which had as its motto, from 1851 to 1853, Mazzini's "God and the People."

The purposes of the Italian Refugee Fund Committee were to secure funds for the many refugees coming after 1848, to respond directly to accusations against Mazzini and the Roman revolutionaries, and to promote the cause of Italian unity. Dickens, who had been an ardent supporter of the Roman Republic, wrote the Committee's Inaugural Address.(47) The Friends of Italy Society was formed to promote the cause of Italian unification in England. Its purpose was twofold -- to explain why the English should have an interest in Italian affairs, and what they could do to help the Italian cause. The Society was to achieve its aims through meetings, lectures, and articles and the use of "all constitutional means" which would "advance the cause of Italian independence in Parliament."(48)

The Society included many of the associates of the Italian Refugee Committee and of the old People's International League. In each of these organizations the membership represented the wide spectrum of Mazzini's British acquaintances. Chartists and Radicals, such as Linton, Holyoake, and Peter Taylor belonged, along with prominent and diverse figures in government and society, including Lord Beaumont, Joseph Hume, and Richard Cobden, and Dickens and William Thackeray. The Council of the Friends of Italy Society included Francis Newman, David Masson, and Arthur Trevelyan.(49)

Mazzini's popularity was the main factor in the support he gained for his movement, but often many of the people who helped him were also advocates of "European freedom" -- the cause of the Poles, for instance, or of the Hungarians. It must be remembered that England was a fertile ground for such causes involving national independence and political or religious freedom. Also the support given Mazzini was not unqualified. Mazzini, through the moderate middle class wing of British radicalism, was working with individuals who would not necessarily support all of his social ideas or even his republicanism.

At the same time, Mazzini was increasingly involved in a struggle with those Italians who especially after the defeats of 1849, had joined in support of Cavour's monarchical program for Italian unification. Mazzini could not repress his republican ideals, but because he was an exile he was unable to gauge accurately Italian sentiment and the state of Italian politics. Many of his followers from Young Italy had already gone over to the "Moderates," as the constitutional monarchists in Italy were called, and in 1857 Cavour backed the founding of the Italian National Society as a rival to Mazzini's revolutionary groups. Its leader was Daniel Manin, a compatriot of Mazzini's and former republican who had served as Triumvir of the short-lived Venetian Republic of 1848.

The antagonism between Mazzini and Cavour was further exacerbated by the Crimean War, 1854-1856, which placed Sardinia and England on the same side with Austria against Russia. For Cavour, this afforded the opportunity to plead Italy's cause before the eyes of the major powers. Mazzini, in contrast, considered the war as an alliance of the Italians and British with despotism. Mazzini was also strongly opposed to the Plombieres agreement reached between Cavour and Napoleon III, which made their nations allies in a coming war with Austria. Mazzini believed that the Italians would be betrayed by Bonaparte, and felt vindicated when in the War of 1859 among the three powers, France at the separate peace of Villafranca, allowed

Austria to keep Venetia, while Sardinia received the region of Lombardy. Cavour considered it a victory in the process of Italian unification. To Mazzini it was a betrayal.

The question of leadership in the struggle for Italian unification was underscored by the visit of Garibaldi to England in 1864. Although Garibaldi had said of Mazzini in 1851 that "he alone has kept alive the sacred fire,"(50) as early as 1856 he too had subordinated his own republican ideals to the belief that only the Sardinian army could drive the Austrians out of Italy, and soon he would come to accept completely the monarchist plan for unification. This served to diminish further Mazzini's reputation in the eyes of those Italians who had already come to look upon the successes of both Garibaldi's forces and of the Sardinian army as proof that Mazzini's strategy of spontaneous republican uprisings would not unite their country. As Bolton King stated, "The republic became impossible on the day, when Victor Emmanuel swore loyalty to the constitution, and thereby proclaimed himself champion of Italian aspirations."(51)

Mazzini had been in Italy, participating in the war, but returned to England for his last exile in 1861. While in England he still tried to influence Italian affairs, secretly negotiating with King Victor Emmanuel II and the Prussian Chancellor Bismarck for a coalition against Austria. But Mazzini's energies at this time were also very much spent in struggles with Marx and with the Russian revolutionary Michael Bakunin for control of both the First International and the Italian workers' movement. Mazzini's debates with these two revolutionary thinkers over the issues of socialism, communism, and nationalism, as well as over what was called the "religious question," were, in a broader context, also debates over widely divergent and competing ideological systems. They were to challenge the validity of principles and doctrines which Mazzini had held all of his life and which he vigorously defended until his death in 1872.

Notes

(1) For biographies of Joseph Mazzini see: Stringfellow Barr, *Mazzini: Portrait of an Exile* (New York: Holt and Co., 1935); Gwilym Griffith, *Mazzini: Prophet of Modern Europe* (New York: H. Fertig, 1970); Bolton King, *The Life of Joseph Mazzini* (London: Dent and Co., 1902); E. E. Y. Hales, *Mazzini and the Secret Societies* (New York: P. J. Kenedy and Sons, 1956).

(2) Giuseppe Mazzini, *Scritti editi ed inediti*, ed. A. Codignola, G. Daelli, E. Morelli, V. E. Orlando, et al. (98 vols., Imola: 1905-1973), 1:9 ("Autobiographical Notes," 1864).

(3) Barr, p. 20.

(4) Alessandro Luzio, *Mazzini Carbonaro* (Turin: Einuardi, 1920), p. 50.

(5) Ibid.

(6) Ibid.

(7) Margaret Josephine Shaen, *William Shaen: A Brief Sketch* (London, 1912), p. 19.

(8) Jesse White Mario, *The Birth of Modern Italy* (London, 1909), p. 10.

(9) Griffith, p. 100.

(10) Mazzini, *Scritti*, 1:317 ("On Historic Drama," 1830).

(11) Joseph Mazzini, *The Life and Writings of Joseph Mazzini* (6 vols., London: Smith Elder and Co., 1898), 3:4 ("Autobiographical Notes," 1862).

(12) Mazzini, *Scritti*, 10:215 ("Notebooks," 1825).

(13) Ibid., 11:358 (letter to Maria Mazzini, April 1, 1834).

(14) Ibid., 4:13 (letter to Maria Mazzini, February 2, 1837).

(15) Ibid.

(16) Ibid.

(17) Ibid.

(18) Ibid., 4:21 (letter to Maria Mazzini, February 25, 1837).

(19) Michael Packe, *The Life of John Stuart Mill* (London: Secker and Warburg, 1954), p. 160.

(20) Mazzini, *Scritti*, 26:127 (letter to Maria Mazzini, December 6, 1837).

(21) King, p. 84.

(22) Barr, p. 130.

(23) Mazzini, *Life and Writings*, 3:324 ("Autobiographical Notes," 1862).

(24) Mazzini, *Scritti*, 30:89 (letter to Maria Mazzini, March 25, 1841).

(25) Barr, p. 143.

(26) Ibid.

(27) Griffith, p. 136-137.

(28) Ibid

(29) Alexander Herzen, My Past and Thoughts, vols. (London: Dent and Co., 1909) pp. 1152-3.

(30) F. B. Smith, *Radical Artisan, William James Linton, 1812-1897* (Manchester: Manchester University Press, 1973), p. 54.

(31) Emilia Morelli, *L'Inghilterra di Mazzini* (Rome: Istituto per la Storia del Risorgimento, 1965), p. 28.

(32) *Hansard Parliamentary Debates*, 3:78:1331-1339 (April 1, 1845).

(33) Ibid.

(34) Morelli, p. 61.

(35) Ibid., p. 62.

(36) Ibid., p. 77.

(37) *Times*, June 15, 1844.

(38) Mazzini, *Life and Writings*, 3:183 ("Autobiographical Notes, 1862)

(39) Ibid., 6:286 ("Address to the Council of the People's International League," 1847).

(40) Smith, p. 76.

(41) Mazzini, *Scritti* 41:78-89 ("Address to the Assemby of the Roman Republic," February 25, 1849), and see Fran]< J. Coppa, *Pius IX*,(Boston: Twayne Publishers, 1979), p. 97.

(42) King, p. 131.

(43) Mazzini, *Scritti* 5:222-256 ("A Letter to Messrs. De Tocqueville and De Falloux, Ministers of France," 1849).

(44) Ibid., 81:167 (letter to E. Venturi, May 1867).

(45) H. W. Rudman, *Italian Nationalism and English Letters* (New York: Columbia University Press, 1940), p. 96.

(46) Mazzini, *Scritti* 54:173-76 (letter to Francesco Crispi, April 25, 1835).

(47) Morelli, p. 116.

(48) Ibid., citing copy in the *Linton Papers*, Istituto Gian Giacomo Feltrinelli, Milan.

(49) Ibid., p. 99.

(50) King, p. 153.

(51) Ibid., p. 155.

CHAPTER II

ST. SIMON, CARLYLE, AND MILL

Among Mazzini's earliest acquaintances in England were Thomas Carlyle and John Stuart Mill. Each of these three thinkers shared, as a common and powerful intellectual influence, the doctrines of Saint-Simon and his followers. As was noted, Mazzini had come to the Saint-Simonian movement in 1832 in Marseilles where he had been close friends with the positivist Demosthene Ollivier. At this time Mazzini was moving away from the influence of the Babouvist disciple and co-conspirator in Paris in 1796, Felipo Buonarroti (1761-1837), and his doctrines of extreme social and economic egalitarianism. The French revolutionary Gracchus Babeuf (1760-1797) had taught a primitive form of communism which also advocated violent revolution as a primary weapon in the class war. But Mazzini, after coming under the influence of Ollivier and the positivists and other French radicals at Marseilles, began to reject Buonarroti's ideas of the inevitability of class war and bloody revolution. Already in 1831 Mazzini wrote that "great revolutions are the work rather of principles than of bayonets, and are achieved first in the moral, and afterwards in the material sphere.(1) Moreover, Mazzini and Buonarroti were further separated by their respective national prejudices. To Buonarroti Paris remained the focal center of the revolution, and he looked back to 1793 with France as the leader of a loosely federated system of egalitarian European republics. Mazzini of course, looked to an Italian initiative for the rest of Europe and stressed Italian emancipation from French ascendancy. The quarrel was also aggravated by the progress of Buonarroti's True Italy organization and its rivalry with Mazzini's Young Italy for the allegiance of the Italian revolutionaries who were in exile. Finally the break between the two became irreparable as a result of Buonarroti's opposition to Mazzini's Savoy expedition.

The Saint-Simonian *Globe* and *Revue encyclopedique*, edited by Pierre Leroux, reinforced ideas that Mazzini had also developed in his youth. Mazzini's political program in 1832 in part reflected this new Saint-Simonian influence.

A republican system is unitary to the extent that it is reconcilable with the greatest latitude for communal and municipal liberty and national sovereignty in government of the country by the country. Popular institutions should tend towards the amelioration of the most numerous and poorest classes, and the abolition of privilege and of all distinctions which are not based on ability and on services rendered by the state.(2)

Here Mazzini combined his republican and nationalist program for Italy, stressing "national sovereignty," with the Saint- Simonian concept of a meritocracy and the idea of "institutions" to ameliorate the conditions of the poorest classes, a point which would be reinforced during his English exile. The Saint-Simonians also had an influence on Mazzini's concept and definition of religion. Mazzini had a strong need to spiritualize all reality, especially the nation. The positivist doctrines of Saint-Simon offered him a way to do this by making the nation -- in Mazzini's case Italy -- the source of a new religion for mankind, a religion that would emanate from the People and replace Christianity as it was spread throughout the world by its followers. Mazzini, also in 1832, defined religion in Saint-Simonian terms: "A faith in general principles that rule humanity, religion is the sanction of the bond that unites the living by the knowledge of a common origin, of a common mission, of a common purpose."(3) And in the Oath of Young Italy, again written in that year, Mazzini underscored these same principles.

Mazzini's discovery of positivism occurred when he was experiencing a grave personal crisis of self-doubt. This crisis reached its peak in 1834 immediately after the birth and subsequent serious illness of a child born to him and his companion Giudetta Sidoli. In his Autobiographical Notes, written in 1862, Mazzini recalled this period of his life:

In those fateful months there grew thick around me such a storm of disasters, delusions, and bitter deceptions, that I suddenly saw in its naked flesh, the growing old of a solitary soul in the world It was also the disintegration of that moral edifice of love and faith within which, alone, I could achieve the strength to fight the scepticism which I saw rising in front of me wherever I looked.

Had that state of mind been prolonged a little, I would have gone really mad or have fallen into.. the egoism of suicide.(4)

But fortunately, he wrote, "one day I awoke with my soul at peace and my intellect serene and the feeling of one who has been saved from an extreme danger."(5)

Mazzini continued to borrow ideas from positivism which he then amalgamated with other systems of thought to develop his own political and social doctrines, as well as a theology to fit his world-view. Saint-Simonianism, especially during the period when Leroux was editor of the *Globe*, helped Mazzini to reinforce the ideas of progress and history which he had already learned from the writings of Condorcet. Condorcet had developed a theory of total history, which he presented in pantheistic terms as the divine unfolding of a pattern of salvation. This concept was shared with Leroux and is found also in the writings of Hegel, Moses Hess, and to some extent Pierre Proudhon.

All of Mazzini's ideas on progress, association, collective humanity, and history are, to a great extent, Saint-Simonian in origin. Each for Mazzini has a teleological or deterministic definition, as it does in Saint-Simonianism. Mazzini understood progress as the "law that God has given to Life, the supreme formula of creative activity, revealed undisputibly by historical tradition." Association -- "the way of progress" -- was based on the "general cooperation and the harmony of work"; and "collective humanity" was the idea that "mankind is a collective entity, in which every generation is bound up with those that preceded and will follow it."(6) Similarly, Mazzini's view of historical periods and events -- the Enlightenment and French Revolution -- closely parallel the Saint-Simonian concepts of critical and organic periods of history, which either initiate or end an epoch. In 1832 he wrote in clear Saint-Simonian terms that "we are at the end of a *critical* epoch and at the beginning of an *organic* one."(7) And, as late as 1852 he stated that the French Revolution was "not a programme it was a resume, it did not initiate, it closed an epoch."(8) For Mazzini the French Revolution was the climax of an historical process which liberated the individual. But being individualistic in its very essence, this Revolution failed to evolve a "unitary concept" to serve as the basis of a new age.

Mazzini believed that, while humanity was ready for that new unifying epoch, such an epoch would only be achieved by the nation as a whole, and not, as the Saint- Simonians thought, by a specific class -- "the producers," or industrial managers, who the positivists thought would initiate a modern productive era for mankind. Ana while retaining the Saint-Simonian plan for a general European Parliament, Mazzini modified another positivist concept which stated that each nation had a unique mission to fulfill towards the progress of humanity. As he envisioned it, "at the head of each [nation] shall be emblazoned the sign of a special mission: upon that of Britain, *Industry and*

Colonies; of the Poles, *Slavonic leadership;* of the Muscovites, *the civilizing of Asia,* of the Germans, *Thought;* of the French, *Action;* and so forth, from people to people."(9) According to this schema, Italy, once independence and unification were achieved, would have the unique mission of revealing to humanity a religion based on progress and association. Mazzini thus reserved for his own country the role of initiator of a new epoch for mankind.

It is because positivism lacked any specific appeal to nationalism, Italian or otherwise, that Mazzini eventually rejected the Saint-Simonian movement. In 1834 Mazzini became familiar with the works of Philippe-Joseph Buchez, a former positivist who had himself already broken completely with the movement, and by the time of his first English exile in 1837, when he had frequent contact with Carlyle and Mill, Mazzini had completely revised his opinion of Saint-Simonianism. One of his chief criticisms at that time to the movement was its inherent utilitarianism -- an objection also shared by Carlyle.

In a series of six articles written for the *People's Journal* in 1846-47, entitled "Thoughts Upon Democracy in Europe," Mazzini traced the common origins of St. Simonians, Fourierists, Owenites, and Communists, whom he took to be the followers of Bentham. They differed in respect to the means -- "the organization that is to ensure the triumph the principles" -- but their principle was the same, utility.(10) He singled out Saint-Simonism as the "boldest and sincerest attempt to carry out the principles of Bentham," for which reason it should never be treated with indifference.(11) In a style reminiscent of Mill's earlier essay on Bentham, Mazzini first praised Bentham for having understood that British society was in great need of reform and for having excelled even Blackstone's efforts to recodify British law. But, like Mill Mazzini identified basic flaws in Bentham's philosophy as the results of a mind more attuned to codifying small details and more fitted to analyzing a single idea than to understanding several ideas at once. Also like Mill, Mazzini found Bentham's greatest error to be a denial of tradition, religion, and history. In his contempt for the past Bentham had completely rejected mankind's common heritage.(12)

Mazzini considered Bentham's philosophy to be the direct antithesis of his own in that it recognized no idea superior to the individual and had no concept of collectivity or association or of a providential plan for humanity. It would have been especially difficult for Mazzini to integrate utilitarianism into his own system of thought because his philosophy was based upon the ideas of the existence of God, collective humanity, unlimited progress, and association. Mazzini cited the views of former St. Simonians, such as Pierre Leroux, who believed that utilitarianism had inspired positivism, with Bentham being the "chief inspirer" of Saint-Simon and among the names most cherished by Saint-Simon's early followers.(13) He added that his own disillusionment with positivism had been strongly influenced by the opinions of Leroux, whom he described as "an ardent St. Simonian before the schism provoked by the morality of Enfantin."(14) Enfantin's bizarre behavior and pronouncement, especially at his "monastery" at Menilmontant, had scandalized many of the Saint-Simonians and caused a split within the movement. Mazzini himself saw Saint-Simonianism's greatest flaw to be the fact that, like utilitarianism, it issued from a single principle, 'the good of all,' and denied the higher principle of liberty.(15) Cautioning against confusing the idea of "utility" with "justice," he revealed the extent to which he had already amalgamated a deterministic sense of history into his own doctrines.

> Again it is said, Justice and Utility are identical: Justice is the idea -- Utility its symbol, its outward sign. By preaching the latter, then, we, by implication preach to the principle. Yes; Justice and utility are identical to the *world*, but not the *agent*.

> In the eyes of all who can penetrate great historical events, the Crusades struck the first blow, at feudalism; they were providentially directed to further the progress of humanity. Does this prove that the thousands of Crusaders who fell by famine and the sword reaped earthly advantage? The fall of the Roman Empire, again, was providentially an advance in the progress of the species ... Can we say that the millions pillaged, crushed, enslaved, would not have a right to protest in the name of Utility against the law of circumstances which imposed martyrdom upon them?(16)

In concluding his critique of positivism and utilitarianism Mazzini mentioned his associate Carlyle, whom he described as "a democrat by every instinctive tendency," but one who "denies democracy a future because he confounded it with the school I am combating."(17)

Carlyle had been introduced to positivism in 1830 when the Saint-Simonians discovered that he was the author of "Signs of the Times" which had appeared anonymously in the June 1829 *Edinburgh Review*. They praised the article's sense of historical periodicity, which they found similar to their own doctrine of critical and organic epochs of history, and the vigor of its critique of existing society. Passages from Carlyle's article were reprinted in the Saint-Simonian *Revue Britannique*, and the movement's missionary, Gustave d'Eichthal, upon learning the author's identity, sent a parcel to Carlyle containing the reviews of "Signs of the Times" and a number of Saint-Simonian publications including *Nouveau Christianisme, Aux Artistes, Le Productuer,* and a translation of Lessing's *L'Education du genre humain*.(18) Carlyle became interested in the movement and he soon wrote to d'Eichthal that he was not opposed to the religious basis of St. Simonianism since it was "the only genuine and permanent basis of all Associations." He praised their motto 'To each according to his capacity, to each according to his works' as the "aim of all true social arrangements," and said that if Saint-Simonianism were presented as "mere scientific doctrine," he could, "with a few reservations subscribe to it."(19)

In 1831 the Carlyles met d'Eichthal, who had been brought to their London home by Mill, and in the following year Carlyle expressed concern over the convictions of the Saint-Simonian leaders Enfantin, Duveyrier, and Chevalier by a French court for immorality and public disorder. By the late 1830's however, Carlyle, like Mazzini, had become disillusioned with the positivist movement, and for similar reasons. Extremism and schisms within Saint-Simonianism had already reached their height. The search for a female messiah in the East, and the development of an elaborate hierarchy, cult, and rituals had consumed the movement and obscured its social and economic doctrines and programs. Concerning this expansion of the movement's "New Christianity" into a hierarchical church, Mazzini wrote that "Humanity had ceased to believe in a Pope and Cardinals and felt no desire to begin again."(20)

Just as the positivist influence can be found in the later writing of Mazzini, it is also evident in the works of Carlyle, especially those written between 1829 and 1841. It is most obvious in "Signs of the Times," *Past and Present*, and *Chartism*. In the last work Carlyle became something of a radical and warned that Chartism was symptomatic of some deeper problem which could not be easily solved by a reform government, or additional troops or police or special funds. These would only would serve to put down the "embodiment of Chartism, without addressing its causes."(21) Throughout *Chartism* Carlyle hammered at the questions of both rights and responsibilities. Like Mazzini, he believed that the laborer has his responsibilities, as does the "captain of industry" (a Saint-Simonian term), and, like Mazzini stated that man's mission on earth was to work. Man would learn his rights and duties through a program of mass education, which both viewed as practical way of creating a more harmonious society.

Some of these similarities are found in Mazzini's own essay on Chartism, "Is It Revolt or Revolution? which also shows the influence of some of Carlyle's earlier works on Mazzini's thought. In this article which was written in 1839 and appeared in 1840 in *Tait's Edinburgh Review*, Mazzini said to the English ruling classes, "Do not get a constabulary and five thousand more soldiers to overawe the Chartists. Instead, he counseled, work with the lower classes and lead them -- Chartism being not some dread portent of the future, but rather "a sign of the times"(22) The main theme of Mazzini's article was that Chartism was symptomatic of some greater moral crisis.

> We must not confound the signs of events that are preparing with the events themselves -- the disorderly, even culpable expression of the feelings that agitate the country, with the feeling itself. Chartism is only a sign -- an expression. The People's Charter will not in my belief, be the Charter of the future. Perhaps of all the topics that it embraces, only one will remain and it is that which represents a principle.(23)

The principle Mazzini referred to was universal suffrage which was a basic tenet of his own republican program. However, he did concur with Carlyle that the question of political organization was entirely secondary, and was merely "a means of realizing that change has matured." (24) Mazzini amalgamated political reform with his own deterministic view of history, advising that while we are not to yield to political innovation for its own sake, we must "not forget that there are necessary, inevitable revolutions, dictated by the eternal progressive march of civilization."(25)

In "Is It Revolt or Revolution?" Mazzini was closer to Carlyle's view in "Signs of the Times" that the events and conditions in England were part of a general European unrest, but whereas Mazzini described the emergence of a "newborn dogma of the People, "(26) Carlyle in 1829 spoke only of "the thinking minds of all nations" calling for a "change."(27) Both Mazzini and Carlyle hated the merely external and mechanical changes of social and political institutions, and sought instead a moral transformation of both society and man himself. In an early chapter of *The Duties of Man*, written in 1844, Mazzini exhorted the workers to improve themselves, because a broad transformation of society would be meaningless as long as they remain with their "present passions and egoism."(28)

But, unlike Carlyle, Mazzini was a political activist and could not base any real changes in the social and political order solely on moral improvement. For Mazzini there had to be some external agent to facilitate man's self improvement, and in the *Duties of Man* he addressed himself to this issue in England. There he again exhorted the working classes to "strive also to instruct and improve yourselves, and to educate yourselves," while acknowledging that "at present this is a labour rendered impossible to the masses in many parts of England."(29) He explained that "a change both in the political and material condition is also needed," and that those who "imagine that an educational transformation may be accomplished alone, deceive themselves."(30)

Mazzini and Carlyle both believed that man found his dignity, identity, and purpose in work. For Carlyle the condition-of-England-question was less a question of poverty than of work, and he sought to elevate the poor by endowing them with the dignity that came only from work. He also saw work as a source of man's spiritual identity, and often described it in religious terms. Mazzini's writings reflect the same sentiment that man is to seek both his spiritual and material identity in his labor.

> The Earth is our Workshop. We may not curse it, we are bound to sanctify it. The material forces that surround us are our instruments of labour, we may not reject them, we are bound to direct them for good.(31)

And in a letter of 1865, he spoke of "the right of work and possession," by which "human nature affirms itself in the physical world."(32) Like Carlyle, Mazzini saw man as defined by his labor, not in the Marxian sense, but rather in the sense that work is the source of man's dignity and rights. But, unlike Carlyle, Mazzini had a teleological concept of work and saw it as both a means through which man participates in the providential unfolding of history and as an individual's link with the rest of humanity.

Mazzini's theories are also evident in the two articles in which he gave his own estimation of Carlyle: "On the History of the French Revolution by Thomas Carlyle" in the January 1840 *Monthly Chronicle*, and "On the Genius and Tendency of the Writings of Thomas Carlyle, which appeared in the October 1843 *British and Foreign Review*. Mazzini's review of Carlyle's *History of the French Revolution* began with a recognition of the author's genius but also noted that other reviewers had overlooked certain inherent dangers in the work.(33) Mazzini did not believe that an event such as the French Revolution could be described in a neutral sense, as Carlyle attempted to do. "The actual state of society is a state of war," the refore no author could be indifferent to such a momentous event.(34) In an exposition of his own theory of history Mazzini explained this further. He felt that every historian must possess his own philosophy of history which should be contained in his works "just as a number contains its own root."(35) But Mazzini's main objection to Carlyle's work, its "capital defect," was the failure to apply any concept of the laws that govern humanity. He criticized Carlyle for recognizing only the individual while failing to demonstrate the role of the "collective life and aim of a people" in history.

Mazzini objected also to the substance of this particular work which he felt failed to correctly analyze the events in France. "Three words remain as summary of the entire history -- *Bastille*, *Constitution*, and *Guillotine*," making it "more properly called *Illustrations of the French Revolution*."(36) Finally Mazzini believed that Carlyle's artistic nature had interfered with his ability as an historian, blaming this on the influence of Goethe whose "evil genius" hovered over the entire trilogy. It was because of this influence that Carlyle had only "contemplated" and not "felt" life. In another article for the *Monthly Chronicle* in 1839, entitled "Byron and Goethe," Mazzini had written a direct response to Carlyle, who had ranked the German ahead of the English poet. To Mazzini Byron exemplified the "internal" and "subjective" forms of individuality which enabled him to understand and experience man's desires, struggles and sufferings, while Goethe as the poet of the "external" and "objective" could only observe mankind with disdain "from the height of his Olympian calm."(37) Mazzini added that he knew of no more beautiful symbol of the destiny and purpose of art, than the death of Byron in Greece.(38)

In his second article on Carlyle, Mazzini again began with praise for Carlyle, noting the effect of "Chartism" and acknowledging that there and in has other works Carlyle had always attempted to deal with the social question. Mazzini extolled his sincerity, idealism, cosmopolitan tendencies, and his humour. But after several pages of such praise Mazzini then noted the one "vital defect" in all of Carlyle's works, the fact that he recognized only the individual while allowing the true sense of the unity of the human race to escape him.(39) Carlyle sympathized with all men, but had no understanding of their collective life. Criticizing Carlyle's theory of the hero Mazzini presented his own interpretation of the "great man" theory of history.

> History is not the biography of great men; the history of mankind is the history of the progressive religion of mankind, and of the translation by symbols, or external actions, of that religion.

> The great men of the earth are but the marking-stones on the road of humanity; they are the priests of its religion.(40)

Mazzini's heroes, unlike Carlyle's or Hegel's, were not the shapers and controllers of history but merely its "marking-stones," or "priests," who moved history one step further according to an already providentially ordained plan.

For Mazzini history was clearly evolving towards a "democratic" future, an "age of the People," and he objected to the contempt that he felt Carlyle demonstrated towards anything that might be termed "political reform."(41) For Carlyle political reforms were secondary to man's moral development, while for Mazzini the two were inseparable Mazzini was also critical of the spirit of fatalism which seemed to pervade Carlyle's *History of the French Revolution*, as well as Carlyle's definition of "duty." "The rule which he adopts is that laid down by Goethe -- 'Do the duty which lies nearest thee.'"(42)

Mazzini saw Carlyle as the man who wants to be a leader, a "man of action," but who has already defined himself as a writer and thinker. "His instincts drive him to action, his theory to contemplation."(43) Mazzini himself faced a similar dilemma and resolved it by choosing both. Like Carlyle he believed that moral and spiritual idealism were necessary components of political and social change. But unlike Carlyle, Mazzini considered himself to be an activist and revolutionary, who, despite his idealism, had no doubt about what he wanted to accomplish.

After 1847, Mazzini and Carlyle, who had met and dined together weekly for nine years, saw less of each other, although Mazzini continued to be a confidant to Jane Welsh Carlyle for some years to come.(44) By the late 1840's Mazzini had become an established figure in British intellectual and radical circles and had earned the respect and friendship of many other leading personalities, including John Stuart Mill. They met in 1837 and Mill soon developed a high regard for Mazzini, praising him in a letter of February 1838, as "one of the most competent" of his associates.(45) In a letter written six months earlier Mill gave his first impressions of Mazzini and an interesting assessment of Mazzini's place in European affairs. He recognized Mazzini as "the most eminent conspirator and revolutionist now in Europe," and an article that Mazzini had just contributed to Mill's *London and Westminster Review* as among the best he had ever received. Mill added that he expected much from Mazzini as a contributor in the future.(46)

The article, "On Italian Literature Since 1830," described in detail the output of Italian literature since that date, and was also a political tract in which Mazzini took the opportunity to introduce his Italian cause to an English audience. "Italy of late," he wrote, in both politics and literature, "has been too much neglected in England." This Mazzini blamed on the silence and indifference of the periodical press, which had caused its readers to believe that intellectual development in Italy had ended with the political failures and frustrations of the 1830's.(47) Mazzini was determined to introduce articles on Italian politics to English journals and reacted strongly to John Robertson, the director of the *Westminster Review*, who found Mazzini's articles too mystical and elevated and urged him to write on entertaining subjects such as "Italian manners, foods, fashions, and bandits."(48) In response Mazzini asked "why should I for the sake of a few sovereigns write articles to make strangers *laugh* at Italy while I *weep*?"(49)

Mazzini's next two articles for the *Westminster Review*, written in 1838, were serious literary and political reviews. "The Lives of Sarpi" concerned the sixteenth century Italian theologian and critic of the papacy, Paolo Sarpi. Sarpi was considered a leader in the struggle against the political aspirations of the popes, and his denunciation of the Inquisition and papal influence over the Venetian republic were stressed in the article.(50) Mazzini praised Sarpi's *History of the Council of Trent,* especially since its anti -papal tone was cons is tent with Mazzini s own view of Italian history, and Sarpi was presented as an important figure in the evolution of a free Italian state. Mazzini's article was still recalled with praise in a letter Mill wrote in 1857.(51)

The second article, "Prince Louis Napoleon Bonaparte," concerned Bonaparte's recently attempted coup d'etat at Strasbourg. After the coup's failure Bonaparte fled to England, and Mazzini, while supporting an attempt against the government that had exiled him, expressed concern that Louis Napoleon's success might have meant a return to Bonapartism. Although described in the article as a man of "courage and capacity,"(52) Bonaparte, after 1849, would become the detested enemy of both Mazzini and Mill.

Mazzini's and Mill's initial association through this series of articles was strengthened by their mutual views on utilitarianism, positivism, women rights, and the question of nonintervention in international politics. For each thinker these issues played an important part in the evolution of their respective philosophies and systems of thought. In his essays "Bentham" (1838) and "Coleridge" (1840) Mill offered a critique of Bentham similar to Mazzini's later essay, "Thoughts Upon Democracy in Europe." Like Mazzini, Mill praised Bentham for his speculation in law and his attention to detail. "He found the philosophy of law a chaos, he left it a science."(53) But then, again like Mazzini, Mill took away his praise for Bentham, and criticized him far reducing all principles to the single idea of utility and for rejecting the past and dismissing all previous knowledge as useless. Mill's criticism that Bentham rejected any truth that was not has own was also paralleled by Mazzini's argument in "Thoughts Upon Democracy" that Bentham belonged to the "eighteenth century school of thought" which had rejected established doctrines but was powerless to replace them with its own philosophy.(54)

While Mazzini made few references to Coleridge, that poet's ideas, especially as presented in Mill's essay, are comparable to Mazzini's. Mill praised Coleridge for being an open-minded, inquiring critic, a seeker after truth in the most positive sense. While Bentham asked "Is it true?," Coleridge pondered "What is the meaning of it?" Bentham was described as one who "stood outside of the received opinion," observing it as a stranger to it, while Coleridge "looked at it from within and endeavoured to see it with the eyes of a believer."(55) To Coleridge the fact that a doctrine had been believed by thoughtful men and had been received by entire nations or generations of men was a part of the problem to be solved.(56)

This question of historical truth had been addressed by Mazzini in 1830 in a two-part article entitled "On the Historical Drama" which he had written for the Italian literary journal *Antologia*. In it he described an "absolute, necessary, and eternal truth" which mankind had been seeking for ages and which was far above "precarious, contingent, and relative" existential facts.(57) Mazzini explained that "truth is one," but "like the rays passing through the prism, it is broken and decomposed, and assumes various appearances in its passage through time and events." He distinguished between historical truth, or truth of facts, and moral truth, or truth of principles the second being to the first as "the whole is to the part, with "facts, principles, all the world contains," all being aspects of truth itself.(58) Mazzini in this essay reiterated Coleridge's view that truth is partially revealed in historical facts, and that man must be a seeker after the truth as it unfolds through the facts and principles of history. In 1861 he reaffirmed this viewpoint in a supplement to the essay in which he wrote that "the idea suggested in these last pages appeared to me at that time, and still appear to me, of great importance."(59)

In his "Coleridge" essay, Mill presented Coleridge's views on civil society, and these too are similar to Mazzini's on that subject. Coleridge believed the requisites for civil society to be "education," "loyalty," and "nationality." Education was defined as a system which "trains the human being in the habit, and thence the power, of subordinating his personal impulses and aims, to what were considered the ends of society."(60) It is a system which provides structure and order to society by preserving society's fundamental principles. Education is "addressed to the moral faculties," without which "equality of duties and of rights is a formula devoid of meaning."(61) In their respective definitions of education Coleridge and Mazzini did not imply a mere system of public instruction, although that is certainly a part of what each proposed for an institution of national education. Rather each envisioned a broad structure which would inculcate the moral values essential to civil society. In the Duties of Man (1844), Mazzini distinguished between "instruction" and "education." He defined education, the cornerstone of his social program, as "the work of nourishment and renewal, which transmits (directly or indirectly) to the individual, the results of the progress of the whole human race." Education would not only guide man towards self-improvement by teaching him "constancy and self-sacrifice," but it would also unite him with his fellowman and create a "noble and powerful harmony" among the various elements of the nation.(62)

Mazzini's statements on education can stand as definitions for Coleridge's institution for national education, the National Church, whose purpose would be "the promotion of a continuing and progressive civilization."(63) The National Church, in Coleridge's view, was not necessarily a religious institution, nor were its members clergymen. Instead they were the 'clerisy' of the nation -- "the learned of all denominations, the sages and professors of the law and jurisprudence, of medicine and physiology, of music, of military and civil architecture" -- in short, the learned of all of the arts and sciences.(64) And, in terms reminiscent of Mazzini's writings on both "duty" and "education," Coleridge's National Church was defined as "the shaping and informing spirit, which educing or eliciting the latent men in all the nations of the soil, trains them up to be citizens of the country."(65)

For his system of national education, Mazzini depended on a "clerisy," the educated classes, to guide their fellow citizens in the educational process. "A few among you, once imbued with the true principles on which the moral, social, and political education of a People depend, will suffice to spread them among the millions."(66) In his essay, "Thoughts Upon Democracy in Europe," of 1847, Mazzini approximated even more closely the structure and intention of Coleridge's National Church. He proposed one central "philosophical" or "religious" institution to which all secondary institutions of instruction and education would be joined. He further proposed that all institutions of higher learning be replaced by "one real apostolate of Knowledge," which would disseminate and popularize the fundamental truth already established by mankind.(67)

Coleridge's other requisites for civil society -- loyalty and nationality -- are comparable to Mazzini's concepts of nationality and association. Coleridge's requisites are defined as "principles of sympathy, not hostility."(68) They are, in fact, nationalism in its most positive sense, and represent a nation's unifying ideals, which are positive because they are not directed against any other nation or people. Coleridge described these sentiments as feelings of "common interest among those who live under the same natural or historical boundaries." (69) It is not "nationality in the vulgar sense," nor is it an "indifference to the general welfare of the human race."(70) Rather, Coleridge explained it as feelings of common sentiment and concern among a people, feelings which he believed were essential to the formation of a nation state.

In the *Duties of Man* of 1844, Mazzini explained nationality in analogous terms, his idea of "association" corresponding to Coleridge's requisite of "loyalty." Mazzini saw the nation as a community of free and equal men, "bound together in fraternal accord to labour toward a common aim"; "it is not an aggregation, it is an association."(71) Before men can associate with other nations, they must have national existence, because It is only in this way that a people can have a recognized collective existence. Each people, each nation, has an historic mission, "assigned by Providence," and thus cannot remain indifferent to the rest of humanity. Finally, linking the requisites of education and nationality with the idea of progress that he derived from the positivists, Mazzini wrote, "The nation is bound to transmit its programme to every citizen," and "every citizen should receive a *course of nationality* -- comprising a summary of the progress of humanity and of the history of his own country."(72)

Although Mazzini closely approximated Mill's ideas as expressed in the "Bentham" and "Coleridge" essays, their views on positivism, and Saint-Simonianism in particular, are somewhat less similar. Mazzini, while retaining such positivist ideas as "progress," "association," and the "unity of humanity," completely rejected the movement itself because of its theological extremism and its inability to detach itself from its utilitarian origins. Also, after 1840, Mazzini would be especially hostile to the positivist thinker Auguste Comte and his followers, believing that Comte had carried utilitarianism to its furthest extremes.

Mill, in his early years, had been enthusiastic about Saint-Simonianism, recognizing like Mazzini, its contributions to the redefinition of political economy. And Mill, even more than Carlyle, had frequent contact and correspondence with d'Eichthal and the other Saint-Simonians who were trying to "evangelize" England. But, by 1837, Mill began to have ambivalent feelings about the movement. As early as 1834 he had become disillusioned with the Saint- Simonian disciples who had come to England seeking converts but instead only exposed the rivalries within their organization. By this time also, Mill sensed the utilitarian nature of the movement, but he still acknowledged the "boldness and freedom from prejudice" with which the Saint-Simonians treated the subject of the family and he admired their teaching of sexual equality.(73) But, for Mill, positivism's greatest flaw was its inherent authoritarianism, the fact that the Saint-Simonians had lost sight of "the values of Liberty and Individuality."(74)

To Mazzini, the French positivist theories were a divergence from his own ideals of duty and progress, ideals which could never be replaced by utility or happiness as the guiding principles of a social order. He gave frequent and strong warnings to the British public about both positivism and utilitarianism, the six articles which comprised "Thoughts Upon Democracy in Europe," being a major example. Through the *People's Journal,* he hoped to reach the working classes whom he believed to be particularly susceptible to utilitarian ideas. Mazzini also feared that positivism's cosmopolitanism, although in many ways similar to his own, might eventually become antithetical to his equally important nationalistic teachings and programs.

Mazzini and Mill both wrote on the utopian socialist movement known as Fourierism, which in some ways resembled Saint-Simonianism. In *Principles of Political Economy,* Mill wrote that of all the forms of socialism the "most skillfully combined and least open to objections is that commonly known as Fourierism."(75) According to its founder Charles Fourier (1772-1837), the operation of industry should be carried out by cooperative units known as "phalansteries." These highly organized social units were to derive productivity from the three elements of "labor, capital, and talent," while maintaining the rights of private property and inheritance. Mill, one of the movement's more favorable critics, added that Fourierism "does no violence to any of the general laws by which human action is influenced," and that it would be "extremely rash to pronounce it incapable of success, or unfitted to realize a great part of the hopes founded on it by its partisans."(76)

Mazzini's analysis of Fourierism is contained in two works: "On Various Social Doctrines: The Fourierist School," 1836, and "Thoughts Upon Democracy in Europe," 1847. In the earlier article Mazzini declared himself in accord with Fourier, especially in his definitions of the origins and nature of the problems of modern society. "The rehabilitation of work," Mazzini wrote in 1836, "is at the basis of all questions of social organization; it is the single and truly fundamental task of political economy."(77) Such a reform, he believed, would end pauperism and replace charity with association. But while Mazzini was in agreement with Fourier and his disciples on this point, he was critical of the fact that Fourier's solutions to the questions of social organization were merely extrinsic. In "Thoughts Upon Democracy" Mazzini told the Fourierists that if they did succeed in reorganizing society into productive units or 'phalansteries, ' itself no easy task, they would be putting in order only "the kitchen of humanity" -- satisfying man's material needs while ignoring the moral ones.(78) And regarding Fourier's scheme for population control which, it was calculated, would reduce two thirds of all women to sterility, Mazzini wrote, "This is Malthus crowned with roses, and pressing the juice of the grape! "(79) In this essay, as in all of his other economic writings, Mazzini upheld the idea of cooperative associations, a principle he shared with Mill and other classic economists. But he insisted that economic reforms, including the development of cooperatives, must also be accompanied by a great moral transformation in man and society itself.

Mazzini and Mill were in closer agreement with each other and with the Saint-Simonians on the issue of women's rights. The Saint-Simonians preached a doctrine of the complete equality of the sexes, with women assigned important positions in the hierarchy of the movement. Mazzini also believed that the questions of equality and female emancipation were of utmost importance, and linked them directly to the issue of the emancipation of the working classes through the idea of education. Because education properly began with the family unit, women were naturally the initial educators of all humanity. Therefore, women's own emancipation had to be a precondition for the emancipation of all citizens, since only those who are completely free can instruct in matters of duties and rights. Mazzini believed so strongly in this that he ended the *Duties of Man* with the final appeal: "*The Emancipation of Women*", then, must be regarded by you as necessarily linked with the emancipation of the Working-man This will give your endeavours the consecration of a Universal Truth."(80)

Mill addressed the issue of women's rights in two essays written in 1851 and 1869, *Enfranchisement of Women* and *The Subjection of Women*. In *Enfranchisement of Women* Mill made an argument similar to that used by Mazzini in the *Duties of Man*. Mazzini admonished the working man to "cancel from your minds every idea of superiority over Women ... you have none whatsoever," and reminded them that such an idea was the result of "long prejudice, an inferior education, and a perennial legal inequality and injustice."(81) Mill too sought to dispel the idea of women`s intellectual inferiority and in *The Subjection of Women* Mill made an appeal to male sensibilities and to the idea expressed by Mazzini that, by limiting women, men are restricting one half of humanity itself, and are thus "adding needlessly to the evils which nature inflicts by their jealous and prejudiced restrictions on each other." (82)

But Mazzini's argument in support of women's rights is actually much broader than Mill's, and is, in fact, grounded in his own definition of the family and its role in the providential formation of the nation. In the *Duties of Man* Mazzini declared that "the family and the country are the two extreme points of one and the same line," and that "the Angel of the Family is Woman." (83) In a passage that recalls the Saint-Simonian doctrine of the "New Christianity, Mazzini explained that "The Mosaic Bible has declared: *God created Man, and Woman from Man;* but your Bible, the Bible of the Future, will proclaim that *God created Humanity, made manifest in the Woman and the Man.*"(84) Here Mazzini went far beyond Mill, who in his arguments for womens rights stressed political issues, such as the suffrage. Mazzini, while arguing for complete female equality, redefined the issue of women's rights in terms of his own plan for a completely new social order. The role of women and the family are intimately linked to his concepts of duty, rights, and the nation, with both women and the family called upon to begin the education of the citizens of his new republican society. Thus Mazzini had to speak of a "Bible of the Future," for like the positivists, he had to reinterpret even traditional religion to achieve his new social order.

The philosopher Gaetano Salvemini has noted that "all the problems raised by Mazzini's teachings lead, sooner or later, to a single problem; what is the place of liberty in this doctrine?"(85) Because Mazzini and Mill both wrote extensively on the subject -- Mazzini in 1858 in the *Duties of Man*, and Mill in 1859 in his essay *On Liberty* -- an analysis and comparison of each of these works offers further insight into Mazzini's intellectual development during his exile.

Mazzini became familiar with *On Liberty* soon after his own chapter "Liberty" was published in *Duties of Man* in 1858. On February 2, 1859, he mentioned Mill's essay in a letter, and a week later wrote, "I am reading *Liberty*. Yes, he is fearless on tyrannicide," but "the definition of Liberty is *arrieree*"(86) The statement on tyrannicide is at the beginning of Mill's second chapter and occurs in reference to the press restrictions in England following the attempted assassination of Louis Napoleon in Paris by the Italian nationalist Felice Orsini in 1858. Mill did not actually argue for tyrannicide, or rather, he was ambivalent about it, but he was opposed to the Government Press Acts which had been passed in England in 1858 as a direct result of the Orsini plot. While Mazzini considered Mill's definition of liberty to be outdated, he was in agreement with Mill's attitude towards tyrannicide because he held similar views and also because this particular attempt was against his enemy Napoleon III. Although he was not a participant in Orsini's plot, Mazzini believed that a successful attempt against Napoleon III would advance the causes of republicanism and Italian unification.

In 1863 *On Liberty* presented a particular problem for Mazzini. Recent political and diplomatic successes had made the program of the Moderates -- the followers of Cavour who sought Italian unification under a constitutional monarchy -- appear, to many Italian nationalists, more pragmatic and much more likely to succeed than Mazzini's rigid and dogmatic republicanism. There were many defections from Mazzini's camp, including his long-time associate Alberto Mario. Mario, in an article on Mill's essay for the Italian nationalist journal *Dovere* used arguments from *On Liberty* to justify the rights of the individual over Mazzini's "Collective Will "If the theory of the mystics gets the upperhand, Mario wrote, "we shall, instead of kissing the slipper of the personal pontiff, kiss that of the collective one."(87) Mazzini reacted sharply, and accused Mario of "inserting in the *Dovere* an article about J. S. Mill, in which he alludes to me as a mystical (sic), and the Duty doctrine as a doctrine of bondage; according to him there is nothing but liberty."(88)

In his chapter "Liberty" Mazzini wrote that "without liberty you cannot fulfill any of your duties, and therefore "you have a right to liberty and a duty too wrest it at all risks from whatsoever Power shall seek to withhold or deny it."(89) He also believed that without liberty there could be no true morality, because man, without freedom of choice, cannot have any sense of responsibility. But he did not envision, even in the most politically free society, as much freedom from societal restraints as Mill did in *On Liberty*. In fact, for Mazzini, liberty itself was the means through which man would achieve harmony with the rest of society. "Liberty is not the negation of all authority: it is the negation of every authority that fails to represent the Collective Aim of the Nation." (90)

In *On Liberty*, Mill argued for just the opposite, for the individual's right to stand outside of society, and even to be in opposition to the majority will or, as Mazzini called it, the "Collective Aim of the Nation." Mill gave as one justification for such liberty the premise that the very existence of truth itself depended on a "collision with error," and that we cannot know truth until it has been tested. "Truth gains even more by the error of one who, with due study and preparation, thinks for himself, than by the true opinions of those who only hold them because they do not suffer themselves to think."(91) This point was so important to Mill that he even argued for the artificial creation of false ideas, so that truth would continue to be tested and thus continually validated. "If opponents of all important truths do not exist it is indispensable to imagine them, and supply them with the strongest arguments which the most skillful devil's advocate can conjure up."(92)

Mazzini, in his essay, also argued for freedom "of opinion upon all subjects," and "liberty of expressing that opinion through the Press, or by any other peaceful means."(93) But, in an enumeration of the various other civil liberties -- freedom of movement, religion, association, labor, trade and commerce -- Mazzini modified his view of freedom of speech and press. While declaring that "the Press must be absolutely free," and that "every preventive censorship is tyranny," he added an important qualification. "Society may, however, punish the errors of the Press, or the teachings of crime or immorality, just as it may punish any other description of error."(94) Mazzini explained that this right of punishment was an important social responsibility, but added also that anterior censorship in itself would constitute "a negation of liberty."(95) Here Mazzini both countered Mill's argument for the necessity of the collision of truth and error and defined the public's right to act against the dissemination of such errors, especially if construed as libelous, criminal, or immoral. He trusted that his proviso against prior censorship would be sufficient to insure the press's freedom.

Mazzini could discuss such restrictions and punishments because, in his enumeration of freedoms -- which are basically political and economic -- he also indicated that the freedoms of "opinion" and "association" were themselves necessary in order to "render that opinion fruitful by cultivation and contact with the thoughts and opinions of others."(96) Thus, he argued for a free exchange of ideas, and even for a certain "collision of truth and error," but still stopped short of Mill's argument for the propagation of error for its own sake. The qualifications Mazzini made in these passages represented his attempts to resolve the problems which arise in a free society when it seeks to define the limits of free speech and the press. Mazzini also understood the dilemma created when all values are subsumed under the single one of liberty. It is in this sense that the following passage from the *Duties of Man* could have stood as a direct response to the central premise of Mill's essay.

> In these later days the sacred idea of Liberty has been perverted by sophistical doctrines. Some have reduced it to a narrow and immoral egotism, have made *self* everything, and have declared the aim of all social organization to be the satisfaction of its desires. Others have declared that all government and all authority is a necessary evil, to be restricted and restrained as far as possible; that liberty has no limit, and that the aim of all society is that of indefinitely promoting liberty, which man has the right of using or abusing, providing his doing so results in no direct evil to others, and that government has no other mission than that of preventing one individual from injuring another.(97)

If Mazzini and Mill took divergent views in their respective essays on liberty, they were much closer in their views on the subject of British non-intervention in international affairs. In 1851 Mazzini published a tract in which he argued that "the principle of Non-intervention in the affairs of other nations is a product of the negative and purely critical spirit of the last century." He explained that it originally had been useful as a policy designed to curb conquest and war which had earlier been part of European politics in the eighteenth century. However, he noted, since that time "the fate of the principle has been peculiar."(98) It had been used, especially after 1815, as a weapon against nationalism, and only in England was the phrase still considered with any degree of respect.(99) It was now time for the English to revise their opinion on the subject.

If a government were despotic and a people resisted it and carried on "a war of the press against it," and despite police and military force defeated it, then the revolution would be legitimate and would have to be accepted as an indisputable fact. No other nation had the right to interfere in the internal affairs of this new government. But should the government of a neighboring despotic state, "either invited by the vanquished party or fearing the contagion of liberal ideas, invade the new state, then the principle of non-intervention would be at an end and all moral obligations on other states to observe it would be nullified. "In other words," Mazzini explained, "the same theory which proclaims Non-interference as the first law of international politics, must include, as a secondary law, the right of interference to make good all prior infractions of the law of Non-interference."(100))

Mazzini applied this theory specifically to the Russian intervention in Hungary, and warned that the British government's insistence on misapplying the principle of non-intervention could indicate that "it is lawful for a Russian Czar to step in, but not at all lawful for the free English people to drag that interfering Czar back."(101) Mazzini also made a similar case for the right of British intervention against the Austrians in Italy. But this argument was not overstated, and actually forms only a small part of the tract. In fact, Mazzini really argued for an international reassessment of the principle of non-intervention itself, making the actual redressing of aggression dependent on the merits of each particular case. He hoped that "new methods of international procedure will be evolved," which will be equally distinct from "a wretched neutrality on the one hand, and from a boisterous military activity on the other."(102) Each case of international aggression or wrongdoing must, be thoughtfully studied and scrutinized so that the appropriate course of action can be determined.(103)

In his essay entitled "A Few Words on Non-Intervention, Mill too dealt with the Russian intervention in Hungary. Published in December 1859, Mill's essay parallels Mazzini's in its argument that any British intervention against the Russians in Hungary would not have been, in itself, a violation of the principle of non-intervention. It would, instead, have been the redressing of a wrong committed by Russia, and would have actually constituted an upholding of the non-intervention principle in international affairs. Mill argued against the Austrian government's right to allow the Russian invasion, explaining that "a government which needs foreign support to enforce obedience from its own citizens, is one which ought not to exist," and that "the assistance given to it by foreigners is hardly ever anything but the sympathy of one despotism with another."(104)

Mill made clear that a nation cannot simply intervene in another nation's civil war, especially in support of despotism, and again like Mazzini, argued for the right of the English government to decide each case on its own merits. Thus, it might not have been correct for the British to intervene initially in the Hungarian struggle against Austrian rule, but once the Hungarians had a clear chance of liberating themselves from Austria, England did have the right, in fact the moral obligation, to prevent a Russian intervention against the Hungarians. It would have been "an honourable and virtuous act" for England to have done this.(105)

Mazzini and Mill both indicted the English, and certainly their leaders, for having encouraged a policy of neutrality. Mazzini's indictment was especially pointed in that lie spoke of the "selfish indifferentism" engendered "by our insular position and our peculiar national occupations," which had become the "sole theory of foreign politics propounded or acted on by many of the public men of England."(106) It is interesting that Mazzini made this appeal in the first person plural, indicating how much he had come to identify with the English by the late 1850's. Mill also condemned the English leaders for their isolationist attitude, and chided them, for the "eternal repetition of this shabby refrain -- 'did not interfere, because no English interest was involved. '"(107)

Finally, both thinkers warned the English of the consequences if this policy were not revised, Mazzini admonishing that "God alone knows if ever the occasion will come that these hirelings of despotism are prepared to march and countermarch even on our own soil of England,"(108) and Mill warning that "the time may not be distant when England, if she does not take this heroic part because of its heroism, will be compelled to take it from consideration of her own safety."(109) In these two relatively little known essays, Mazzini and Mill came closest in their respective political thinking. Each looked to England to redress the balance of power in the interests of her own security as well as in the interests of liberal and nationalist causes on the continent. Certainly, Mazzini would have supported any British intervention in Italy against the Austrians which might have helped his own republican movement. But the theme of his tract on non-intervention is much broader, because like Mill, he believed that England, more than any other nation, had the responsibility to act against an advance of despotism wherever it occurred in Europe.

Mazzini kept his friendship for Mill all of his life, and at one point, in 1858, was one of the few people invited by Mill and Harriet Taylor to that reclusive couple's home at Blackheath.(110) In the same letter containing this invitation, Mill discussed with Mazzini their mutual disdain for Napoleon III and their opposition to Lord Palmerston's bill which permitted the arrest and imprisonment of foreigners in England who had conspired to assassinate foreign rulers abroad.(111) This bill had also been inspired by the Orsini plot against Napoleon III. In another letter that same year Mill, in phrases reminiscent of both *On Liberty* and "A Few Words on Non-intervention, cautioned Mazzini about the English people themselves. Referring to an unnamed projects of Mazzini's, Mill reminded Mazzini of the English indifference to foreign affairs, their rejection of the idea of equality, and the fact that they "keep what sympathy they have for those whom they look upon as imitators of English institutions."(112)

Mazzini's and Mill's other letters contain many references to their mutual respect and esteem for each other, and, although not meeting together for some years, Mazzini closely followed Mill's two election campaigns in 1865 and 1868. His friendships with both Mill and Carlyle were important factors in his intellectual life in exile, and these friendships helped sustain him during the decades when lie experienced political defeat abroad. Although after 1844 he had a closer working relationship with the British radicals and Chartists, he continued to bring to his writings and policies the intellectual experiences that were the consequence of his contact with Mill and Carlyle, the central figures in the first years of his English exile.

Notes

(1) Giuseppe Mazzini, *Scritti editi ed inediti*, ed. A. Codignola, G. Daelli, E. Morelli, V. E. Orlando, et al. (98 vols., Imola, 1905-1973), 2:124 ("Manifesto of Young Italy," 1831).

(2) Ibid., 3:18 (letter to Sismondi, 1832).

(3) Ibid., 1:362 ("Thoughts on the Poets of the 19th Century," 1832).

(4) Ibid., 72:248-251 (Autobiographical Notes, 1862)

(5) Ibid.

(6) Joseph Mazzini, *The Life and Writings of Joseph Mazzini* (6 vols., London, 1898). 4:passim ("The Duties of Man," 1858).

(7) Scritti, 2:124 ("On the Various Causes Which Have Hitherto Impeded the Development of Liberty in Italy," 1832).

(8) Mazzini, *Life and Writings*, 3:215 ("Europe: Its Conditions and Prospects," 1852).

(9) Ibid.

(10) Ibid, 6 : 98 ("Thoughts Upon Democracy in Europe, 1846).

(11) Ibid., p. 128.

(12) Ibid., p. 129.

(13) Ibid.

(14) Ibid.

(15) Ibid., p. 131.

(16) Ibid., pp. 134-135.

(17) Ibid., p. 139.

(18) Richard Pankhurst, *The Saint Simonians, Mill, and Carlyle* (London, 1960), p. 29.

(19) Ibid, p. 33, citing *The New Quarterly*, 1909, 2:279-288.

(20) Mazzini, *Life and Writings*, 6:101 ("Thoughts Upon Democracy," 1846).

(21) Thomas Carlyle, *Selected Works, Letters, Reminiscences*, J. Symons, ed. (Cambridge, 1970), p. 259-260, "Chartism" (1839).

(22) *Scritti*, 22:400 ("Is It Revolt or Revolution?," 1840).

(23) Ibid., p. 392.

(24) Ibid., p. 375.

(25) Ibid.

(26) Ibid.

(27) Symons, *Carlyle*, p. 43 ("Signs of the Times" 1829).

(28) Mazzini, *Life and Writings*, 4:227 ("Duties of Man," 1844).

(29) Ibid., p. 233.

(30) Ibid.

(31) Ibid.

(32) *Scritti*, 70:211 (letter to Moncure Conway, 1865).

(33) Mazzini, *Life and Writings*, 4:110 ("On the History of the French Revolution by Thomas Carlyle," 1840)

(34) Ibid.

(35) Ibid. p. 126.

(36) Ibid. p. 118.

(37) Ibid., 6:97 ("Byron and Goethe," 1839).

(38) Ibid.

(39) Ibid., 4:56 ("On the Genius and Tendency in the Writings of Thomas Carlyle," 1843) .

(40) Ibid., p. 78.

(41) Ibid., p. 96.

(42) Ibid., p. 102.

(43) Ibid.

(44) Thomas Carlyle, *Reminiscences*, J. A. Froud, ed. (London, 1881), p. 75.

(45) John Stuart Mill, *Collected Works,* Francis E. Minek, ed (24 vols Toronto, 1963), 13: 378 "The Earlier Letters, 1812-1848." (letter to the Secretary of University College, February 13, 1838).

(46) Ibid, 17:1978 "The Later Letters, 1848-1873 (letter to Sir William Molesworth, September 22, 1837).

(47) Mazzini, *Scritti,* 28:161 ("On Italian Literature Since 1830," 1837).

(48) Ibid., 27:155 (letter to Maria Mazzini, October, 1838).

(49) Ibid.

(50) Ibid., 31:78 ("The Lives of Sarpi," 1838).

(51) Mill, "Later Letters," p. 534 (letter to Pasquale Villari, June 30, 1857).

(52) Mazzini, *Scritti*, 31:137 ("Prince Louis Napoleon Bonaparte," 1838)

(53) John Stuart Mill, *Bentham and Coleridge*, F. R. Leavis, ed. (London, 1962), p. 103.

(54) Mazzini, *Life and Writings*, 6:128 ("Thoughts Upon Democracy in Europe," 1847).

(55) Mill, *Bentham and Coleridge*, pp. 121-122.

(56) Ibid.

(57) Mazzini, *Life and Writings*, 2:80-96 ("On the Historical Drama," 1830).

(58) Ibid.

(59) Ibid.

(60) Mill, *Bentham and Coleridge*, p. 136.

(61) Mazzini, *Life and Writings*, 4:84 ("Duties of Man," 1844).

(62) Ibid.

(63) Mill, *Bentham and Coleridge*, p. 152. Citing S. T. Coleridge, "Church and State," chp. 5.

(64) Ibid.

(65) Ibid.

(66) Mazzini, *Life and Writings*, 4:90 ("Duties of Man," 1844).

(67) Ibid., 6:107-108 ("Thoughts Upon Democracy in Europe," 1847).

(68) Mill, *Bentham and Coleridge*, p. 122.

(69) Ibid., pp. 124-125.

(70) Ibid.

(71) Mazzini, *Life and Writings*, 4:227. ("Duties of Man," 1844).

(72) Ibid.

(73) John Stuart Mill, *Autobiography*, J. J. Cross, ed. (London, 1924). p. 148.

(74) Ibid.

(75) John Stuart Mill, *Collected Works*, ed. J. M. Robson, Book 2, *Principles of Political Economy*. (Toronto: University of Toronto Press, 1965), p. 212.

(76) Ibid., 2:213.

(77) Mazzini, *Scritti*, 7:403. ("On Various Social Doctrines: The Fourierist School," 1836)

(78) Mazzini, *Life and Writings*, 6:168. ("Thoughts Upon Democracy in Europe," 1847).

(79) Ibid., p. 170.

(80) Mazzini, *Life and Writings*, 4:377-378. ("Duties of Man", 18-t1)

(81) Ibid., p. 284.

(82) John Stuart Mill and Harriet Taylor Mill, *Enfranchisement of Women*, and John Stuart Mill, *The Subjection of Women* (London, 1983), citing *Subjection of Women*, p. 187.

(83) Mazzini, *Life and Writings*, 4:282. ("Duties of Man," 1844).

(84) Ibid., p. 290.

(85) Gaetano Salvemini, *Mazzini* (Stanford: 1957), p. 92.

(86) *Scritti*, 63:170. (letter to Emilie A. Hawkes, February 2, 1859).

(87) Ibid., 74:185. (Excerpt from Albeto Mario, "John Stuart Mill's 'Liberty, *Dovere*, February, 1863) -

(88) Ibid., 74:185. (letter to Caroline Stansfeld, May 1, 1863).

(89) Mazzini *Life and Writings*, 4:306-307. ("Duties of Man," 1858).

(90) Ibid., p. 311.

(91) John Stuart Mill, *A Selection of His Works*, John M. Robson, ed (New York: 1966), p. 94. "On Liberty."

(92) Ibid.,p. 95.

(93) Mazzini, *Life and Writings*, 4:310 ("Duties of Man," 1858).

(94) Ibid., p. 311.

(95) Ibid.

(96) Ibid., p. 310.

(97) Ibid., p. 313.

(98) Mazzini, *Life and Writings*, 6:300. ("A Tract on Non-Intervention," 1851).

(99) Ibid., p. 301.

(100) Ibid., p. 305.

(101) Ibid., p. 306.

(102) Ibid., pp. 307-308.

(103) Ibid.

(104) John Stuart Mill, *Essays on Politics and Culture*, Gertrude Himmelfarb, ed (New York: 1962), p. 380. ("A Few Words on Non-Intervention," 1859).

(105) Ibid., passim.

(106) Mazzini, *Life and Writings*, 6:301. ("Non-Intervention," 1851).

(107) Mill, *Essays on Politics and Culture*, p. 371. ("A Few Words on Non-Intervention, 1859).

(108) Mazzini, *Life and Writings*, 4:306. ("Non-Intervention," 1858

(109) Mill, *Essays on Politics and Culture*, p. 384. ("Non-Intervention," 1859).

(110) Mill, "Later Letters," 15 518. (letter to Joseph Mazzini, February 21, 1858).

(111) Ibid.

(112) Ibid., 15:552-553. (letter to Joseph Mazzini, April 15, 1858).

CHAPTER III

THE CHARTISTS AND RADICALS

During the first period of his exile, when Mazzini was in frequent contact with Mill and Carlyle, he became acquainted with several of the leading figures in the Chartist movement. Among these were William J. Linton, William Lovett, and John Cleave. Cleave was a radical bookseller, who, along with Lovett and others had founded the London Workingmen's Association in 1836; he was also the distributor of the journal Mazzini began for Italian workers in England, the *Apostolato Popolare.(1)* In 1841, when Mazzini established the Italian night school, he met Lovett whose neighboring coffee shop was a frequent meeting place for Chartists and emigre revolutionaries, and the same year he was also introduced to Linton by his physician, the noted aurist, Joseph Toynbee. (2)

But Mazzini's interest in Chartism actually predated these friendships. In 1838 he closely followed the circulation of the National Petition and the course of the movement itself. In August of that year, he mentioned a meeting at Birmingham led by "a big industrialist, [Thomas] Attwood."(3) In September he referred to another where Henry Vincent and others had been chosen as leaders, but added that he expected little from this leadership, because all Englishmen were "materialists, utilitarians, and benthamites 'par excellence (4) However, a month later Mazzini was more sympathetic and wrote to his family that he had again gone to a Chartist meeting and heard "an [Ebenezer] Elliot, an iron worker and popular poet, full of merit, and one whose name is on the lips of all the workers"; he now described Vincent as a "young worker who speaks with a singular fluidity."(5) He also observed that the absence of the middle classes from these meetings irritated the workers because it made them feel more isolated in their struggle.(6)

Later letters of December 1839 and the early months of 1840 recount in detail the trial of the Chartist John Frost, the leader of the violent Newport Rising of November 1839. Mazzini wrote that both the trial and the Queen's wedding preoccupied the English, and at the end of the trial expressed his own hopes that Frost's sentence would be commuted as part of an amnesty in honor of the royal wedding.(7) Mazzini followed the case until the government commuted the sentence to transportation for life, but noted that Frost had been taken away without being able to see his wife and family first.(8)

Shortly after his arrival in London, Mazzini served as a correspondent for two liberal continental journals, the Paris based *Le Monde* and the Swiss

Helvetie, in which he gave lengthy analyses of social and political conditions in England as well as his first impressions of the "popular element" and the politics of the working classes. His initial article for *Le Monde* began with an analysis of the Reform Act of 1832. He described the Act as "all wrong and incomplete," but nonetheless important because it was both a break with tradition and a means through which "the mind of the people" could be expressed.(9) It was significant as the first step, however small, towards a democratization of the British government. The Whig party was dying, but its death would not profit the Tories who would also fail because, since 1830, their party had been dominated by "concessions, betrayals, and terror, and above all by an imprudent audacity."(10) The English were divided into "two distinct nations," "the parliamentary" and the "non-parliamentary" or "unrepresented," and one day the "unrepresented" would actually come before Parliament demanding recognition.(11) Those members of Parliament, such as John A. Roebuck, who supported the Charter were men of "conscience and democratic franchise," as well as, "radically speaking, the most advanced."(12)

In articles for the Swiss journal, *Helvetie,* Mazzini gave his early impressions of radical politics in England. In October 1838 he described his own arrival in London, a stranger in the country, his interest aroused by the little that the French papers have revealed of the British political clubs, their meetings, and of the popular associations.(13) However, the English papers said nothing of these activities. "In Parliament, in the journals and newspapers which cover the world, you hear only of Whigs and Tories, Lord Melbourne and Sir Robert Peel: pure questions of *power* and not of *principles.*" While representatives of the working classes met periodically at the 'Crown and Anchor' tavern, nothing of these meetings was mentioned in the "high-placed" press.(14) England was a nation ready for revolution, because, while individuality is sacred and enjoyed by all, it was surrounded by hunger and ignorance, as all wealth was concentrated in one end of the social spectrum while the other was weighed down by immense poverty.(15)

In this series for *Helvetie* Mazzini wrote of the "popular element" in terms reminiscent of Engels, describing its "consciousness of itself," which went unnoticed by the rest of the nation. "The people live, suffer, and complain, but this complaint, like their suffering, is unheard, they are born and die in their places."(16) While the popular element had its press, its newspapers, its meetings, it had no voice which reached the rest of the nation. One might spend a long time in London without ever meeting this "frightening element," and might think that one had seen everything, when in fact, one only had wandered about "one of the circles of the London hell."(17)

Other indications of Mazzini's growing interest in English radical politics are found in his correspondence in 1838 and 1839. Writing to an associate on Malta in early 1838 Mazzini spoke of English radicalism as having two forms, the "parliamentary" and the "extra-parliamentry."(18) The first represented only the middle classes and proceeded "by *steps* and not by *principles*." It had neither "faith, boldness, leadership," nor "enough heart to sustain a newspaper.'(19) The other form, the "extra-parliamentary," had "faith, boldness, activity." but lacked money, influence, and leadership. However, it did have a weekly journal, and, because it sympathized with republicanism, it would be ready to declare fraternity with other people who were in rebellion. Radicalism, although without fixed doctrines -- "today Lamennais, tomorrow Babeuf and the men of '93" -- would, once it found leadership, grow and produce a revolution. Such an event, however, would be far off, "because things go slowly here."(20)

Later, in July 1839 Mazzini told of the Bull Ring Riots in Birmingham. The riots occurred when the city sent police to break up a regular Chartist gathering which was being held in its customary place at the Bull Rings. The resulting riot led to destruction of property and the calling in of troops. Lovett, Vincent, and other leading Chartists were present. In a rather exaggerated account Mazzini described the mob as "tumultuous, killing policemen, robbing houses, and threatening arson." These were forms of protest which he could not condone but could understand, because all peaceful and legal means of petition had been treated so far not only with refusals but with contempt. He predicted the outbreak of a bloody revolution, which, because it would be social as well as political, would be "worse than '93."(21) By November 1839 Mazzini had completed the draft of his essay "Is It Revolt or Revolution?" This insightful analysis of both Chartism and radical politics was based not only on his long discussions with Carlyle, Mill, and other "respectable" members of society, but also on first-hand observations of the movement and his acquaintance with the leadership that would guide Chartism through the early 1840's.

When Linton met Mazzini in 1841 he was, like many other Chartists and Radicals, attracted to Mazzini's charismatic personality and his commitment to republicanism and political reform. It was because of this that Linton immediately ranked Mazzini with Lammenais as a leading thinker of the age. Mazzini himself soon introduced Linton to two other important exiles in

London, Stanislaus Worcell and Karl Stolzman, and it was these four, along with Lovett and the Chartist Henry Hetherington, who were thrown together in 1844 in the "Post Office Espionage" case, in which the Home Office revealed the contents of Mazzini's mail to the Austrian authorities. The subsequent parliamentary debates and wide publicity of the case made Mazzini the best known political exile in England. A significant result of this incident was Mazzini's open letter to the Home Secretary, entitled "Italy, Austria, and the Pope," which was published in serial form in the *Northern Star* beginning in September 1845. Mazzini analyzed the various governments ruling in Italy, with the Austrian presented as the most despotic and the Papal as the most corrupt. Comparing conditions in Italy with those in England he concluded that because basic rights and freedoms already existed in England but not in Italy, violent revolution was a justifiable alternative only in the latter country.(22) This was the first statement of an opinion he was often to reiterate, that because the freedoms of speech, press, and assembly, as well as an active role of public opinion already existed in England, conspiracy and insurrection there would be both dangerous and counter-productive. The Italians, on the other hand, having "neither Parliament, nor hustings, nor liberty of the press, nor liberty of speech, or possibility of lawful public assemblage" with which to attain political change, had the right to resort to violent revolution.(23)

Clearly, Mazzini by 1845 had revised, if not his view that England still needed important political changes and that the Chartist demands were justified, at least his perception that the people were without a voice and that revolution in England was a viable alternative. This change of mind also corresponded to that of most Chartists and radicals at the time who drew similar conclusions for the same reasons. In Mazzini's case, both his vindication in the Post Office Espionage Case, which proved that English institutions guaranteed the rights even of foreigners, and his continued contact with "moral force" Chartists and other "moderates" among the British radicals helped to bring about this re-evaluation. Mazzini was also well aware of the help that a wide basis of British support could give to his Italian cause and of the freedom that he had been given, as an exile in England, to propagate that cause both at home and abroad. He saw no reason to alienate the respectable elements of British society which had so strongly supported him in 1844 and who were already well disposed towards the cause of Italian nationalism.

It is significant that Mazzini's essay in the *Northern Star* served to uphold the views of the "moral force" Chartists who held that political change in England must come about peacefully through the existing institutions and by changes in public opinion. Mazzini however, had no illusions about this paper's influence beyond the working classes. Two months before the article appeared, he wrote that while the *Northern Star* had a large circulation, it was exclusively among the working classes. Consequently, the paper did not have "any influence among the upper classes, among the classes that count."(24)

The division within Chartism over the question of the use of "moral" or "physical" force as a political strategy was reflected, after 1844, in the founding of several international societies by the leaders of each of these factions. Lovett began the first such society in London in 1845, the Democratic Friends of All Nations, a "moderate" organization which included, at least nominally, many of the leading continental exiles. Soon after, the militant George Julian Harney founded the Fraternal Democrats which quickly replaced Lovett's as the leading international organization in London. The Fraternal Democrats were vaguely communistic and unconditionally supported physical force as a weapon, at least on the continent. But this organization's communism and egalitarianism were, in principle, unacceptable to Mazzini.

For this reason, and because he saw the need for a moderate organization which would carry out his goals in England, Mazzini founded the People's International League in 1847. It superseded Lovett's Democratic Friends as the moderate international society in London and chief rival of the Fraternal Democrats. The League was also the first popular association in England with a primary objective of influencing that country's foreign policies. Linton served as secretary and the executive committee included prominent Chartists, like Thomas Cooper and James Watson, as well as such "respectable" members of British society as Joseph Toynbee and Thomas Duncombe, the Member of Parliament who first brought Mazzini's petition before the Commons in the Post Office Espionage case. Other members of the League were the Chartist leader Henry Vincent, W. J. Fox, a leading orator of the Manchester School, and Peter A. Taylor, a Radical member of Parliament for Leicester. By bringing together moderate Chartists and important British radicals, the League gave Chartism a new focus after its defeats in the mid-40's. There was, of course opposition to the League from the Fraternal Democrats and "physical force" Chartists who believed that the League held up only middle-class English freedoms as examples to European nations. These same freedoms, Harney said, were the cause of distress in England, and the "physical force" Chartist Ernest Jones warned others to stay away from the League altogether.(25) But though Harney had no use for the League, he did not attack Mazzini personally and, in fact, usually invited Mazzini to important meetings of his Democratic Committee for Poland's Regeneration, and Mazzini's articles were always gladly welcomed in the *Northern Star* which Harney at that time edited.

The League attracted the support of the "moral force" Chartists, who although they had reservations about supporting violent European revolutions, were sympathetic to those who were in rebellion. The People's International League helped them out of this dilemma by allowing them to declare that violence was the only means that Italians, Poles, or other oppressed peoples had to free themselves, while British workers had recourse to peaceful means to attain their rights. Certainly Mazzini was skillful in advocating revolution on the Continent without offending either "moral force" Chartists or middle-class followers. The publications of the League, which were never far removed from Mazzini's drafts, spoke of Europe as a "sleeping volcano" and identified the "will of the people" with the "will of God." But the English were urged only to "welcome" and "hail" nationalistic uprisings, and, as both oppressors and oppressed would use force anyway, to encourage their government to give support to the side of the oppressed.

> There is no thought in this of any armed intervention in the affairs of Europe, no thought of England embroiling herself. Let her only speak out firmly and decidedly: her voice will be listened to ... Her present apathy encourages aggression, and so does more than aught else to make the sword the sole arbiter of right. It is emphatically for Peace that the League is founded.(26)

In 1851 Mazzini founded the Friends of Italy Society which had much the same general program as the People's International League, but devoted its attention to Italy. The Society's headquarters were in London with branches in the provinces. Here radicals, Chartists, and members of the establishment all took part in an organization which Mazzini hoped would advance the Italian cause in England, and it was in this interest that Mazzini published one of his more eloquent essays, "Europe: its Condition and Prospects," in the *Westminster Review* in 1852. This article was written primarily to counter the demands of European governments that political refugees be expelled from England and sent to America. These governments,

Mazzini said, falsely maintained that only a few agitators, inspired by the ideas of the French Revolution, were responsible for all political unrest on the Continent. The truth instead that subversive movements had originated among the masses. Consequently, Mazzini urged that Europe be reorganized along strictly national lines, and that England, in the interest of the balance of power, should protect these new nations from outside aggression.(27) And since the European problem involved social as well as national questions, he restated his desire for a more equitable distribution of income among the classes.(28)

More than any other continental exile, Mazzini was accepted by Chartists of various factions. He enjoyed the support of a secularist such as Holyoake, contributed to Harney's *Northern Star* and *Red Republican*, and still maintained a wide basis of support and influence among other radicals. His influence in the Chartist press also greatly increased after 1845. In 1846, for example, Linton's *People's Journal* published a series of articles by Mazzini, "Thoughts Upon Democracy in Europe," warning the English working classes of the dangers of utilitarianism and communism. Although this series was Linton's most brilliant catch for his journal, he felt compelled to edit parts of the second article in which Mazzini spoke favorably of Christianity and the doctrines of salvation and eternal reward. Such ideas were anathema to Linton and the journal's editor John Saunders, but because Mazzini insisted that the passage remain, Linton added a footnote dissociating the paper from these particular sentiments.(29)

This series was followed by several other articles for the *People's Journal* on the political situation on the Continent. The first of these, written in 1847 and entitled "Cracow," dealt with the recent Austrian annexation of Cracow into Hapsburg domains, an event which signaled the official disappearance of Poland as a sovereign country.(30) Despite this annexation, Mazzini wrote, the Poles would remain as a people and one day would arise to reclaim their nation.(31) He linked the cause of the English workers with that of the European nationalists, saying that the strongest support in England for European nationalism was actually among the working classes. "Let them say what they will of the English government, but let the name of Englishman be respected and loved by the oppressed of all nations."(32) In later articles he reiterated these views on Poland and also declared that Russia's mission of civilization lay only to the East.(33) In his second article that year, "The European Question," another appeal for English support of European nationalism, Mazzini predicted the revolutions of 1848.(34) Later articles in

1847 dealt with the question of nationalism as well as with the questions of utilitarianism and collectivist doctrines.(35)

Mazzini was also influential in establishing a relationship between English and Continental radicalism. It was he who, in 1848, brought Linton to Paris to greet Lammenais and leaders of the new revolutionary French government; this helped reinforce the influence that French thinker had on radical and republican thought in England. Mazzini, was also partly responsible for the popularization of Lammenais' ideas among the Chartists, with Harney, for example, naming his *Friend of the People* after one of Lammenais' journals and later including him in his calendar of "republican saints."(36)

When, in 1848, Linton launched has new paper, the *Cause of the People*, with Mazzini s motto "Ora e Sempre" on its masthead, it too became a vehicle for Mazzini's ideas. In 1850 Linton traveled to the Continent to meet Mazzini at Lausanne where he was in hiding after the defeat of the Roman Republic and was given letters of introduction by Mazzini to Aleander Herzen in Paris and political tracts to distribute. Consequently, Herzen joined Mazzini as a contributor to a new radical English journal, the *Leader*, which began that year. By this time Harney had moved closer in his views to Linton, being convinced by Mazzini that the Chartists needed a sense of republican fraternity if they were to have any influence in the struggle for the suffrage in England. Mazzini's ideas are evident in the *Democratic Review* which was begun by Harney in 1849 and featured articles by other revolutionary nationalists including Alexandre Ledru-Rollin and Arnold Ruge.

In 1850 Harney and Linton founded the *Red Republican* in which Mazzini's series "Royalty and Republicanism in Italy" was published. It occupied up to three of the eight pages of each issue. Mazzini's theme was the advancement of the republican cause in Italy and the linking of that cause with the general European republican movement He argued that because Europe was advancing so rapidly towards democracy, the most logical form of which was the republic: a republic must be "one of the *facts* of the future", consequently, "if the Italian revolution desires to strengthen itself by an Alliance with the European popular movement it must be republican."(37) But while advocating support for such movements on the Continent Mazzini did not openly espouse the cause of English republicanism. There are several reasons for his reticence. As a foreign exile, he would be naturally cautious about any statements concerning a republican revolution in England and would not wish to offend a government that had offered him refuge since 1837. Nor would he want to alienate the more respectable members among his British followers who, while supporting the Italian cause, would have grave reservations about a republican movement at home. Moreover, although he still viewed England as a nation that was in need of significant social and political reforms, he had by this time, developed a better understanding of the stability and uniqueness of British institutions. Thus Mazzini anticipated a view that he would come to accept fully by the early 1860's -- that the British might be the one exception to his republican ideal.

That Mazzini's ideas had an important influence on English republicanism is evident in the writings of both Harney and Linton in the *Red Republican* and afterwards in Linton's *English Republic*. Taking "liberty," "equality," and "fraternity" as their starting point, both writers redefined these concepts in Mazzini's distinctive terms. Liberty became organic liberty, "the growth of all" based on natural law, in contrast to the "selfish" liberty of the Enlightenment. Equality was not the "equal condition of all men -- as dreamed of by some Socialists, but rather that condition created by universal suffrage in which "the law made by all may care for all -- that all are treated equally." And fraternity was amended to "humanity, specifically following the example of Mazzini in the *Duties of Man*.(38)

Other articles by Mazzini in the *Red Republican* and *English Republic* developed his themes of the sacred role of the family and equality of the sexes, the inviolability of personal property, the desirability of free trade in land, state education, universal suffrage, and European republicanism and international government Engels, who was carefully following the course of British radicalism, was sufficiently concerned about Mazzini's influence to write to Marx that "the humbug which Harney is carrying on with Mazzini and Co. is getting too bad," and advised that Harney would have to be put back "on the right track."(39) By the "right track" Engels implied that Harney, who had a tendency to support indiscriminately any form of revolutionary ideas and to admire "official great men," should eschew his friendship with Mazzini and other emigre figures and join Marx and himself in their relatively isolated political existence.(40) Engels also told Marx that he planned to send articles to the *Friend of the People*, successor to the *Red Republican*, which would be specifically designed, under the guise of commentaries on continental events, to discredit Mazzini and his followers.(41)

Perhaps the clearest transposition of Mazzini's ideas into English occurred in Linton's *English Republic*, founded in 1851. In articles dealing with duty, republicanism, socialism, universal suffrage, and the status of women, there appeared passages which distinctly recall Mazzini's remarks on these subjects in the *Duties of Man*. In reference to duty, for example, Linton wrote, "As right is universal, so is duty ... There is no such thing as rights without duty. Humanity -- human life -- is one."(42) Similarly, republicanism was linked with the issue of equality of the sexes. "Truth is of no sex. Republicanism embraces the whole of Humanity. Humanity is man and woman."(43) And in an essay on education Linton called for a system of compulsory education based on instruction in the arts and sciences as well as in the "use of arms" and in the "divine laws of duty." There was also mention of a State Church which would embrace and educate citizens of all denominations.(44) Other articles from the *English Republic* which seem to have been inspired by Mazzini, whom Linton praised as having a nature which "perfectly combined" the practical with the poetic, spoke of the rights of private property, the institution of social credit, cooperation between labor and capital, and the establishment of a citizens' militia so that England would be able to intervene in the "world-wide war between peoples and governments for nationality."(45)

The line of descent of Mazzini's teachings in English radical thought, which originated in Linton's journals, continued through the writings and sermons of Linton's disciple, the radical Birmingham preacher George Dawson.(46) Since the late 1840's Dawson had been an ardent supporter of Mazzini and his teachings and it is through him that the influence of Mazzini's ideas can be traced to Kineton Parkes, the publicist of Ruskin's social teachings in the 1890's and the editor of a later edition of the *English Republic* in the Swann Sonnenschein series of socialist texts.(47) Through Parkes, in turn, these same ideas were then further disseminated, contributing ultimately to the development of late nineteenth century English aesthetic and puritan radicalism.

Linton himself was to have a lifelong admiration for Mazzini and for his "God-like teachings, making his journey in 1856 to New York, for example, in large part because Mazzini had asked him to help revive support and raise funds for the Italian cause in the United States. Linton worked diligently at this project for over a year.(48) Such devotion on the part of Mazzini's English followers was not unusual.

Another instance of the high esteem in which Mazzini was held by Chartists and Radicals was his long association and friendship with the freethinker George Jacob Holyoake. Holyoake, who was a member of the Friends of Italy Society had been an early supporter of Mazzini and despite the fact that Mazzini was a decided theist, welcomed him as a frequent and important contributor to his secularist journal, the *Reasoner* (19) In that journal, which began in 1816, Holyoake published original articles by Mazzini and reprinted others including *Faith and the Future* which had appeared in 1850. While the *Reasoner* was primarily a journal of free-thought, it also sought to prepare the workingman for a greater role in public affairs, and for this purpose Mazzini's articles were most useful. Although in many sections of *Faith and the Future*, some of which were written as early as 1835, Mazzini made frequent references, to religion, the work was basically an exhortation to the working classes to join in a republican movement that would herald the beginning of a new epoch of history. Because *Faith and the Future* was both an affirmation of republicanism and of a "religion of Humanity," Holyoake believed that he could incorporate segments of the work into the *Reasoner* while still maintaining the journal's secularist integrity. In fact, the *Reasoner*'s audience tolerated Mazzini's continuance as a contributor to the journal more because of his prestige among the radicals and the popularity of the Italian cause than for such statements as: "Believe and act, that which Christ has done, humanity can do."(50) To Mazzini, collaboration with free-thinkers was justified, because, as he wrote to Holyoake, "We pursue the same end -- progressive improvement, association, transformation of the corrupted medium in which we now live."(51) Recognizing their respective philosophical differences, he explained to Holyoake that he saw his own political mission in religious terms. "All that we are now struggling, hoping, discussing, and fighting for, is a religious question."(52)

Holyoake's *Reasoner* also became a vehicle for the Italian cause. In 1852, Holyoake printed and distributed a broadside appeal from Mazzini for shilling subscriptions to a fund supporting Italian nationalism -- the subscriptions deliberately set at a shilling limit so that the working classes could participate. And, in 1855, the *Reasoner* raised £450 for one of Mazzini's undertakings and comparable funds later for projects such as Garibaldi's invasion of Sicily.(53) In 1857 Holyoake published, as a pamphlet, Mazzini's "The Late Genoese Insurrection Defended," which its addressed to the British Radical Joseph Cowen, Jr. of Newcastle In this tract Mazzini gave his explanation for the failure of an attempted republican rising at Genoa the year before which resulted in the death or capture of several Italian nationalists.(54) He denied charges that he had destroyed the peaceful liberty of the independent Italian Kingdom of Piedmont which then controlled Genoa, arguing that Piedmont itself, satisfied with its own prosperity and freedom, had turned its back on the cause of Italian unification. At the end he repeated his familiar theme that the only hope for unification was through the republican movement.(55)

Through the *Reasoner*, Holyoake continued to be a lifelong supporter and fundraiser for Mazzini, and in 1858 Mazzini praised him for having the courage to publish the pamphlet by the French revolutionary Felix Pyat, "Tyranny and Tyrannicide," in the aftermath of the attempt by the Italian revolutionary Felice Orsini to assassinate Napoleon III in January of that year.(56) Perhaps one of the strongest statements of Mazzini's respect and friendship for Holyoake was has letter in 1864 apologizing to Holyoake for the conduct of a fellow Italian. Mazzini expressed his sense of "humiliation for Italy" because of his countryman's misconduct and assured Holyoake of his own esteem, affection, and gratitude for his efforts on behalf of the Italian cause.(57)

During the 1850's Mazzini sought to extend his basis of British support beyond the area of London into the provinces. The Friends of Italy Society had, by 1851, established chapters in other parts of Britain where Mazzini made three important new converts to his cause : John McAdam, a wealthy Glasgow pottery-maker, William Rees, a noted Welsh preacher and poet, and Joseph Cowen, Jr., the son of a leading industrialist from Newcastle. Each was to play a part in the dissemination of Mazzini's ideas and the popularization of the Italian cause among the British. McAdam, who was Mazzini's major contact in Glasgow, had been involved in reform movements since 1832, when he organized the massive North-West demonstration held on Glasgow Green. Shortly afterwards he emigrated to America, where he remained until 1847. On returning he became involved with various emigre nationalists including Mazzini, Louis Kossuth, Karl Blind, Louis Blanc, and others. But McAdam was most devoted to the Italian cause and became one of its leading propagandists, organizing several large meetings at Glasgow during the 1850's in support of British intervention in Italy. At these rallies lie often encountered opposition from the followers of Bright and the Manchester School who supported a policy of pacifism in the interests of free trade.(58) McAdam also advised Mazzini about British public opinion regarding the Italian cause.

In the course of their twelve year correspondence Mazzini frequently commented on Italian affairs and often sought McAdam's assistance. In 1858 lie candidly admitted to McAdam that he "fully recognized the improbability of having help in England for a republican Italy." But, he added, because "monarchy leads only to an unavoidable economic and moral bankruptcy," the time has come for a "radical change" in Italy.(59) Even the success of the Savoy monarchy in furthering the cause of Italian unification could not convince Mazzini to abandon his republican principles Mazzini, more optimistically, told McAdam in 1861 that the new government in Piedmont, which came to power upon the death of Cavour, was doomed to failure and would soon collapse. He also stated his belief that Cavour's death would allow new opportunities for military actions against Rome and Venice by Garibaldi and his forces.(60) Later, in 1864, Mazzini told McAdam of his hopes for a possible Italian alliance with Bismarck against Austria and France stressing that the British would find an anti-French alliance advantageous to their own foreign policy goals. He instructed McAdam to organize meetings in support of such an alliance and reminded him that a "bold general manifestation of British opinion" against Napoleon III's advances in Italy might also help to prevent the Mediterranean from becoming "a French lake." (61)

McAdam was of additional use to Mazzini when, through the Garibaldi Italian Unity Committee, founded in 1859, he served as an important link between Mazzini and Garibaldi. This was at a time when Garibaldi's popularity among the English was growing while Mazzini's was somewhat on the decline. Mazzini constantly exhorted McAdam to raise funds and supplies for Garibaldi's volunteers in Italy, and later sent him as part of the delegation to Garibaldi conveying Mazzini 's personal invitation to visit England.(62) The visit, which took place in 1864, proved crucial to the revitalization of interest in the Italian cause among the British, and also served to strengthen temporarily the ties between Mazzini and Garibaldi.

Typical of the devotion that Mazzini inspired among the British for himself and his movement was that of the Welsh preacher, journalist, and national poet, William Rees Although Rees only met Mazzini in 1860, he had long been his admirer and between 1845 and 1853 had published several articles and delivered many sermons in support of Italian nationalism. After 1860, Mazzini often called upon Rees to help raise funds and gather support for the Italian cause in Wales.(63) "Esteemed as you deservedly are by your country men and lecturing as you do before large audiences, you can and will do a great deal of good to our National Cause," Mazzini wrote him in 1861. Warning him of the dangers of the French presence in Italy, Mazzini expressed the hope that a general European outcry as well as a suspension of the British policy of non-intervention, would force the French troops out of Rome.(64) Like many of Mazzini 's supporters, Rees was quite willing to carry out Mazzini's directives and worked faithfully to rally support for the Italian cause among the British. Rees has especially important to the cause because, through his sermons, lectures, and in his Welsh national newspaper *Yr Amserau* ("The Times"), he helped to establish a basis of support for Mazzini beyond England and the major British cities.

Outside of London, English support for Mazzini was especially strong in the North. In Newcastle the wealthy industrialist Joseph Cowen, Jr. was one of Mazzini's more ardent collaborators. Cowen, who was also an associate of Harney and other Chartists and radicals, first became acquainted with Mazzini in 1845, when, as a student at Edinburgh, he wrote to Mazzini offering his assistance to the Italian School in London. Cowen was a republican in the tradition of Mazzini and lie him was a moralist. Both attitudes are reflected in his writings. "Capital has its duties as well as its rights, and there ought to be closer than a mere money-bond between "'masters' and men. '"(65) As a supplier of weapons to the republican forces in Italy, he also fit Mazzini's model of the person who "harmonized thought and action." (66) In 1854 Cowen, with editorial help from Harney, began the *Northern Tribune*, a monthly in which lie presented both his own ideas and those of Mazzini In this short-lived journal --- it lasted less than a year -- he published Mazzini's views on such matters as universal suffrage and republicanism.(67) For both Mazzini and Cowen the ideal republic was a type of latter-day Athens, based upon duties and virtue rather than social equality. Cowen remained a republican in this sense, in contrast to Harney, for whom "republic" meant a social as well as a political democracy. But while Cowen completely accepted Mazzini s definition of a republic he differed with Mazzini over other important issues, especially those concerning the Crimean War.

When the Crimean War began in 1854 it was enthusiastically greeted by most British radicals as an opportunity to help free the oppressed peoples of Eastern Europe from the tyranny and ambitions of Czarist Russia. There were, of course, exceptions. Cobden and Bright and the followers of the Manchester School, for instance, opposed hostilities as bad for trade. Mazzini too was against the war, but for a very different reason. In his view, Austria's diplomatic support of the allies after December 1854 drastically changed both the nature and purpose of this conflict. For moral and political reasons he would not endorse a British alliance with Austria, the common oppressor of Hungary and Poland as well of as Italy, and this is why he vehemently attacked the coalition that Great Britain and Piedmont had formed with Austria against Russia.

In a "Letter to the English People on the Crimean War," published in the *Morning Advertiser* on March 23, 1855 Mazzini claimed that there was a great misunderstanding between the people and the government as to the objectives of the Crimean War. The people believed that they were fighting for "civilization, for liberty, against the spirit of absolutism; for the independence of nationalities against the encroachments of despotism."(68) The government, on the other hand, was fighting for. the 'status quo,' trying to maintain what was extant of the Europe of 1815 and to prevent nationalities from rising. The people knew that they had nothing in common with Austria, while the government persisted in sacrificing many lives for the "phantom" of an Austrian alliance. The English people wanted "a free and united Italy," but their government, which twice before had betrayed that country, was now, through the Austrian alliance, aiming "the deadliest blow at the national Italian party by allying Piedmont with Austria."(69)

The separation of the English people from their own government, Mazzini explained, came about because there was no link between them, "no regular permanent channel, through which the former can act in *due time* on the latter."(70) Secrecy shielded all international transactions, so that before the people could speak, the government had already acted. The will of the English people was ignored by their government in matters of foreign policy because the leaders of government, although chosen by the people, were not selected from among them. Thus the people could blame, and even punish the mistakes of their leaders, but they could not change the leaders themselves. Before offering help to oppressed nations, the English should consider healing the divisions within their own country. Such a task, while not impossible, would be difficult, because although there existed few direct political obstacles, there was a "certain half-despairing, half-selfish, moral inertness, which had grown parasitically on your souls, and cramped your old Saxon vigour."(71) This condition was the result of the "practical atheism" of the English, a lack of faith or religion which would have linked "thought with action." It was necessary to fight against this because any nation that could, in one instance, speak of the freedom of Poland and Hungary, and, at another moment, enter into an alliance with Austria did not deserve to win a war.(72) The Crimean War, which was immoral and without principles and purpose, should have been "a war of liberty against European despotism," or at least one that was fought in defense of the principle of non-intervention; the latter would have inspired the oppressed nationalities to rise up and join the allies. In return for the alliance, England had received nothing from Austria, not even military help, thus making the possibility of victory even more difficult.(73)

Mazzini added that he was speaking not as an Italian but as a friend of England, his "second country." That some Englishmen shared his sentiments is suggested by the response to his letter. The editor of the *Daily Telegraph*, Alfred B. Richards, an outspoken opponent of Cobden and the Manchester pacifists, used Mazzini's words to attack the Austrian alliance which, he said lined England with its enemies against those who were her actual friends, the oppressed nationalities (74)

Mazzini continued his attack on the war in a second open letter published in the *Daily News* in July 1855. Here he concentrated on the sacrifices of the soldiers, who although they continued to fight, could never win without a radical change in the government's policy.(75) Just as the Piedmontese in 1848 had failed to take advantage of risings in Lombardy to thwart the Austrian advance there, so had the English missed their opportunity in this war to encourage insurrections in Eastern Europe which might have weakened the Russians behind their own lines Because of this the war became a bloody state of siege in which England would bear the biggest burden. "The youth of England shall be periodically decimated for no other purpose than that of gratifying the military ignorance of Louis Napoleon, and withdrawing every source of alarm from the Austrian government."(76) This military strategy seemed determined to "sink in an apparently plausible enterprise the best blood of England, and make her defenseless for a time of need."(77) It was not in the Crimea that England had to fight, but rather in Poland, the one area where Russia was vulnerable, and where neither Austria nor Prussia would interfere. "Leave Prussia to its people; Austria to the Hungarians and to ourselves ... Czarism is a principle, the principle of unbounded authority; it is only a principle -- that of universal liberty -- that can conquer it."(78) At the end of July Holyoake published both of these letters in a pamphlet entitled "Two letters to the People of England on the War," contributing further to the controversy over the war and provoking the charges of David Urguhart a former diplomat and M.P. who was also a fanatical Russophobe, that Mazzini was actually a Russian agent in disguise.(79)

Mazzini's opposition to the war was shared by the leaders of the Manchester school, Cobden and Bright, but for very different reasons. While Mazzini saw the alliance of both England and Piedmont with Austria as a betrayal of the ideas of liberty and nationalism and a perpetuation of Austrian rule in both Italy and Eastern Europe, the free-traders of the Manchester school opposed the war for the purely economic reason that it disrupted trade. Mazzini was, in principle, opposed to all forms of pacifism, including that of the Manchester liberals, and in 1856 his views on the subject were made clear in a controversy with the Italian nationalist Daniel Manin over the question of the use of force, specifically the act of assassination, in attaining political objectives. Manin, who as a former republican who had come to accept Cavour's plan to unify Italy under the Savoy monarchy, had also come to believe that it was actually Mazzini and his violent republican strategy which were the main obstacles to Italian unification. In a letter to the *Times* in 1856, he labeled such revolutionary strategies as "theories of the dagger, denouncing them as the greatest threat to Italian national aspirations.(80)

While Mazzini was not specifically mentioned by name, the reference was understood, and he indignantly replied in an open letter to Manin. Although such "theories of the dagger" never existed in Italy, he wrote, there were rare occasions when assassination could be considered correct -- "exceptional moments in the life and history of nations, not to be judged by normal rules of human justice, and in which the actors can take their inspiration only from their conscience and God.(81) Tyrannicide was justifiable when it was the only viable means of ending an intolerable oppression. If it was commonplace to glorify Judith, Brutus, and Charlotte Corday for committing tyrannicide, it would be hypocritical to condemn those who, in the same spirit, tried to kill Louis Napoleon or Ferdinand of Naples. In general, however, he abominated political assassination as a crime, especially when attempted with the idea of revenge, when other means to attain freedom were available, or when it was directed against a man "whose tyranny does not descend to the grave with him."(82)

Manin's indictment against Mazzini was aimed also at the use of force in popular insurrections. Here Mazzini's response was more straightforward. It was nonsense, he said not to call murder a soldier's shooting of his enemy, while so labeling the stabbing, by an artisan conspirator, of an Austrian soldier with the only weapon that was at hand.(83) Circumstances in Italy made both "irregular," or guerrilla, warfare and assassination the only viable alternatives that the Italians had against repressive foreign regimes. Unfortunately, the example lie used, of the stabbing of the papal minister Rossi in 1848, somewhat weakened his case because that assassination, although committed in revolutionary times, was actually inspired by political revenge.(84)

In 1864 the controversy over Mazzini's encouragement of tyrannicide was revived when Disraeli, in the House of Commons, accused Mazzini, not without some justification, of organizing from England assassination plots on the Continent. Disraeli, who had earlier denounced Mazzini's tactics as "ensanguined practices," now charged that Mazzini had involved members of the government in a plot against Napoleon III. James Stansfeld, Mazzini's long-time friend and supporter, who had just become a Junior Lord of the Admiralty, had allowed Mazzini to use has home address for foreign correspondence. When this connection was revealed Disraeli castigated Stansfeld for his friendship with a conspirator.(85) Bright came to Mazzini's defense, citing lines from a poem written by Disraeli himself in support of tyrannicide.(86) As a result of the controversy Stansfeld was forced to resign from the government and Mazzini once again became a public figure, having again precipitated a Cabinet crisis.

During his exile in England Mazzini reiterated and clarified other ideas that he had held since his youth, especially the economic theories that he had incorporated into his social program for a republican state. In 1847 he wrote that among the economic problems a republican democracy had to solve were: a complete transformation of the tax system, the establishment of a state economy, an increase in production, a progressive abolition of all but the indispensable intermediaries between buyer and seller, and a union of capital and labor by means of workingmen's associations.(87) To achieve these goals Mazzini set forth certain economic axioms. First, although the right of private property must be maintained, the state should try to equalize fortunes through taxation. Property was necessary to stimulate labor and encourage ingenuity. "The man who works and produces has a right to the fruits of his own labour; in this resides the right of property."(88) Next, the establishment of the new social organization must not be achieved by compulsion. Voluntary organization was a preliminary step to any lasting social advancement, and his own economic projects depended on voluntary societies for cooperative production. Finally, the objective of any plan for economic change must always be an increase in productivity. There could be no change in the workers' conditions unless national productivity was increased. Throughout has works Mazzini consistently argued for high wages because they would stimulate demand, which, in turn, would cause an increase in production that would gene rate further wage increases.(89)

Mazzini himself had many general suggestions for economic improvement. He proposed free trade in land; legislation to protect tenants, arbitration between capital and labor, compulsory national insurance, and regulation by the state of the stock exchange, as well as guaranteed employment for all citizens.(90) For Italy, he suggested a broad plan of home colonization on unreclaimed lands, although he failed to take into account the pervasive problem of malaria in such areas. Also, surprisingly, he opposed emigration which later proved to be a chief factor in relieving unemployment. But essentially Mazzini's program rested on the two proposals of a radical reform of taxation and the development of voluntary cooperatives. Regarding tax reform Mazzini proposed that all indirect taxes and special taxation on land be abolished and replaced with a strongly graduated income tax.(91) Although he supported free trade he was somewhat ambivalent about the repeal of the Corn Laws in England, at times seeming to support the Chartist position which stated that repeal would lower wages, while at others arguing for the benefits of repeal.(92) In either case he castigated the Manchester liberals, who were the leading opponents of the Corn Laws, because he believed that they had brought England to its "egoistical" position by "materializing" all economic questions.(93)

Mazzini's plan for cooperative production appeared in its basic form as early as 1833, but he worked it out in more detail in the later years of his life. It was based upon the same principle of association which he applied to his social and political programs. For the economic aspect of this idea he proposed the accumulation of a large reserve of national funds. This reserve was to be obtained by the nationalization of church lands, railways, mines, and some unspecified "great industrial enterprises."(94) The question of compensation remained unclear. The income from these sources, and from the rents of reclaimed lands and from properties which lapsed to the state, would form the "National Fund," or "tax of democracy," whose main purpose was to be the financing of voluntary industrial and agricultural cooperative societies. Any society that could outline its goals and capabilities was to have a claim on the fund, with only minimal interest to be collected on its loan. The repayment was to be to special banks administered by communal councils. The societies were to be given absolute freedom of the management, sale, and disposal of net income.(95) They were to have the right to deposit unsold produce in national storehouses, in exchange receiving negotiable notes that could serve as currency. Finally, the cooperative societies would be given the opportunity to compete with private firms for government contracts.(96) But the rest of Mazzini's economic program is rather general and tend to be lacking in details. In fact, he disliked economic studies, and stated that a real understanding of economic questions was to be found "in the workshops and homes of the artisans" rather than in "statistics and documents" which were always incomplete and tended either to conceal or exaggerate economic ills.(97)

Mazzini consistently posited that any system of political economy, and especially his own program for economic reform, must be established within a morally revitalized society. Such a society could only come about through political reforms and a moral transformation of the people themselves, achieved through a comprehensive system of national education. It was this moral purpose that led Mazzini to support Chartist and radical movements during his first decade of exile, and that inspired the various organizations that he founded in support of European nationalism and republicanism. After 1863, in his last period of exile, He would again use this moral interpretation of political and economic questions as important arguments in his struggle with both Marx and Bakunin for leadership of the First International and control of the workers' movements in Italy and England.

Notes

(1) Mazzini, *Scritti*, 19:330 (letter to Maria Mazzini, November 11,1840).

(2) William Lovett, *Life and Struggles* (London, 1876, reprint ed. London: MacGibbon and Hee, Ltd., 1967), p. 72.

(3) Mazzini, *Scritti*, 7:158 (letter to Luigi Amadeo Meligari, August 24, 1838).

(4) Ibid., 7:186 (letter to Maria Mazzini, September 15, 1838).

(5) Ibid., p. 189 (letter to Maria Mazzini, September 25, 1838).

(6) Ibid., 18:303 (letter to Maria Mazzini, December 11, 1839).

(7) Ibid.

(8) Ibid., 18:362 (letter to Maria Mazzini, February 2, 1840).

(9) Ibid., 17:42 ("Correspondence to *Le Monde*," April 4, 1837).

(10) Ibid., p. 44.

(11) Ibid.

(12) Ibid.

(13) Ibid., 17:186 ("Correspondence to *Helvetie*, October 19, 1837).

(14) Ibid., 17:191 ("Correspondence to *Helvetie*," October 26, 1837).

(15) Ibid.

(16) Ibid., p. 199.

(17) Ibid., p. 201.

(18) Ibid., 18:409 (letter to Nicola Fabrizi, January, 1838).

(19) Ibid.

(20) Ibid.

(21) Ibid., 18:118 (letter to Maria Mazzini, July 18, 1839).

(22) Mazzini, *Life and Writings*, 3:197-262 passIm. ("Italy, Austria, and the Pope," 1845).

(23) Ibid.

(24) Mazzini, *Scritti*, 28:67 (letter to Maria Mazzini, July 19, 1845).

(25) *Northern Star*, September 25, 1847, p. 8.

(26) "Address of the Council of the People's International League," June 22,1847, Cowen Collection, Central Reference Library, Newcastle.

(27) Mazzini, *Life and Writings*, 6: 215-265 passim. ("Europe: Its Conditions and Prospects," 1852).

(28) Ibid.

(29) *People's Journal*, April 17, 1847 and Frederick W. Hoenig, ed, "Letters of Mazzini to W. J. Linton, *Journal of Modern History* (1933), 5:58-60 (Mazzini to Linton, April, 1847).

(30) Mazzini, *Scritti*, 34:66 ("Cracow, 1847)

(31) Ibid.

(32) Ibid.

(33) Ibid., p. 243 ("On the Slavonian National Movement," 1847).

(34) Ibid., p. 205 ("The European Question," 1847).

(35) Mazzini, *Life and Writings*, 6:187-197 passim. ("A Few Last Words Upon Fourierism and Communism," 1847).

(36) G. D. H. Cole, *Chartist Portraits* (London: Macmillan and Co., 1941), p. 268.

(37) Mazzini, *Life and Writings*, 5:48 ("Royalty and Republicanism in Italy," 1850).

(38) "Letter I: Republican Principles," *Red Republican* George Julian Harney, ed., September 21, 1850, pp. 110-111. Reprint ed., London: Merlin Press, 1966.

(39) Karl Marx and Frederick Engels, *Briefweschel*, 4 vols. (Berlin, 1929), 1:141-146 (letters of Engels to Marx, February 5, 12, 1851).

(40) Ibid.

(41) Ibid.

(42) *The English Republic*, Kineton Parkes, ed. (London, 1891) pp. 104-123.

(43) Ibid.

(44) Ibid., p. 81.

(45) Ibid., pp. 62-66.

(46) R. W. Dale, "George Dawson: Politician, Lecturer, and Preacher," *Nineteenth Century*, v. 2, August 1877, pp. 45-6.

(47) Kineton Parkes, *English Republic*; "William James Linton," *Bookman's Journal and Print* Collector (July 8, 1921) and Walter Crane, *An Artist's Reminiscences* (London, 1907).

(48) William J. Linton, *European Republicans: Recollections of Mazzini and His Friends* (London, 1892), p. 180 and William J. Linton, "Some European Republicans," *Century Illustrated Monthly Magazine*, April, 1886, pp. 407-411.

(49) George Jacob Holyoake, *Sixty Years of an Agitator's Life*, 2 vols. (London, 1902), 1:91; and George Jacob Holyoake, *Bygones Worth Remembering*, 2 vols. (London, 1906), 1:125.

(50) Mazzini, *Life and Writings*, 3:79 ("Faith and the Future," 1835).

(51) Mazzini, *Scritti*, 54:186 (letter to George Jacob Holyoake, April 9, 1855).

(52) Ibid.

(53) Holyoake, *Sixty Years of an Agitator's Life*, 1:266.

(54) Mazzini, *Scritti*, 40:167 ("The Late Genoese Insurrection Defended," 1857).

(55) Ibid.

(56) Ibid., A5: 270 (letter to George Jacob Holyoake, March 25, 1858).

(57) Joseph Mazzini to George Jacob Holyoake, April 22, 1864, George Jacob Holyoake Collection, Cooperative Union, Ltd., Holyoake House, Manchester.

(58) John McAdam to Joseph Cowen, Jr., March 11, 1859, Cowen Collection, Newcastle-upon-Tyne Central Library, Newcastle-upon-Tyne.

(59) Joseph Mazzini to John McAdam, April 20, 1858, John McAdam Collection, Glasgow University Library, Glasgow.

(60) Joseph Mazzini to John McAdam, June 12, 1861, McAdam Collection.

(61) Joseph Mazzini to John McAdam, April 15, 1864, McAdam Collection.

(62) John McAdam to Joseph Cowen, September 1, 1860, Cowen Collection.

(63) Piero Rebora, "Lettere di Mazzini ad un Predicatore Gallese," *Nuovo Antologia*, 218, (1922), pp. 130-134.

(64) Joseph Mazzini to William Rees, February 6, 1861, William Rees Collection, National Library of Wales, Aberystwyth.

(65) *Northern Tribune*, 1, February, 1854, p. 63.

(66) E. R. Jones, *The Life and Speeches of Joseph Cowen* (London, 1885), p. 86.

(67) *Northern Tribune*, 1-20, 1854-1855, passim.

(68) Mazzini, *Life and Writings*, 6:310 ("Two Letters to the English People on the Crimean War, Letter I," 1855).

(69) Ibid. p. 315.

(70) Ibid.

(71) Ibid., p. 323.

(72) Ibid.

(73) Ibid.

(74) *Morning Advertiser*, March 27, 1855.

(75) Mazzini, *Life and Writings*, 6:328 ("Two Letters to the English People on the Crimean War, Letter II," 1855)

(76) Ibid.

(77) Ibid. p. 330.

(78) Ibid. p. 334.

(79) Mazzini, *Scritti*, 54:220 (John Alfred Langford, "Mazzini, Urquhart and the Conferences," with a letter from George Dawson, London, 1855).

(80) *Times*, February 1, 1856, p. 20.

(81) Mazzini, *Life and Writings*, 6:266-284 ("On the Theory of the Dagger, 1856).

(82) Ibid.

(83) Ibid.

(84) Ibid.

(85) *Hansard Parliamentary Debates*, 5, lxxv, March 17, 1864.

(86) Ibid.

(87) Mazzini, *Life and Writings*, 6:214 ("Thoughts Upon Democracy in Europe," 1847).

(88) Ibid., 4:209-366 ("Duties of Man," 1844-1858).)

(89) Ibid., passim.

(90) Ibid., and 6:220 ("Thoughts Upon Democracy in Europe." 1847).

(91) Ibid. 4:209-366 ("Duties of Man," 1844-1858)

(92) Mazzini, *Scritti*, 28:265 (letter to Maria Mazzini, January 13, 1846).

(93) Ibid., 78:258 (letter to Peter Taylor, June 1, 1858).

(94) Mazzini, *Life and Writings*, 4:209-366 ("Duties of Man," 1844-1858).

(95) Ibid., passim.

(96) Ibid.

(97) Ibid., p. 259.

CHAPTER IV

MARX AND BAKUNIN

Long before the polemics with Marx and Engels for control of the First International had begun Mazzini had been following the developments of both socialism and communism. As noted by Salvemini, Mazzini was one of the first writers to use the word "socialism," observing, for example in 1834, that his new movement was "destined to constitute humanity in the form of socialism."(1) But by this Mazzini meant only a regulation of the economy through producers' and consumers' associations. His social radicalism, which was what his socialism amounted to, never included the concepts of class struggle or the abolition of private property. In fact, when socialism became more revolutionary Mazzini no longer associated the term with his own economic program. In 1844 he wrote, "We are not communists, nor levelers, nor are we opposed to the ownership of property, nor socialists in the sense given to the word by a sectarian school of thought."(2) He believed that if the doctrines of collectivization and state control of all means of production and distribution were implemented, society itself would be paralyzed and all citizens reduced to "the level of bees and beavers."(3) Fortunately, he added, such concepts were confined, at least in England, to only a section of the workmen, "the saner and more intelligent portion [being] far from such follies"(4)

In 1846 in "Thoughts Upon Democracy in Europe," Mazzini condemned communism as the worst of all the systems that had been derived from the utilitarian tradition because it sought to abolish at once religion and the family as well as freedom itself.(5) It was the insistence upon absolute equality in the distribution of goods which made communism basically tyrannical and, by upholding a false conception of equality, also deprived man of the higher value of liberty while reducing him to a "cypher."(6) Once in control, communists would display the same intolerance as religious fanatics who proclaimed that any truth which was contrary or extraneous to their own teaching was dangerous and must therefore be forbidden.(7) Other errors of communism included the abrogation of the ideas of the family and the nation. While it was true that each of these institutions were imperfect, abolishing them would rob man of his very identity, for it was through the family and the nation that an individual received both stimulus and relief from his labors. A final proof that communism was a bankrupt system was the fact that it had never produced a "single vigorous thinker" within its ranks.(8)

Mazzini's critique provoked responses which he answered in June 1847 in the *People's Journal*. In "A Last Word Upon Fourierism and Communism" Mazzini repeated his objections to both forms of collectivism, and explained to his English critics that they would be mistaken to equate communism only with non-violent systems, such as Owen is, or to think that ultimately any system which denied property and individuality would not end in tyranny.(9) Instead, Mazzini recommended the development of workers' associations which, because they were voluntary and recognized private property, were compatible with democratic institutions. Again expressing his faith in the good sense of the English people, he borrowed a phrase from Carlyle, suggesting that they would regard communism as merely another "Morrison's pill for universal happiness."(10) Mazzini added a critique of Proudhon --"the Mephistopheles of Socialism" -- to the Italian translation of the same article in 1864 when he was engaged in polemics with Proudhon's followers for control of the First International.(11)

In his early writings on communism, Mazzini took little notice of Marx himself. In 1852 in "Europe: Its Conditions and Prospects," he did attack the *Communist Manifesto* but in veiled terms, noting that socialism would fail tactically because it alienated the petty bourgeoisie and drove the bourgeoisie to reaction.(12) Referring directly to communism, he repeated his belief that, with the exception of Marx, "who was desirous of being the chief of a school at any price," there was no one else who thought that the communist system could be established simply by enactment.(13) This was, of course, exactly the opposite of Marx's intentions. But if at this time Mazzini was mistaken about Marx and communism, in a later and more insightful analysis he observed that Marx was "a man of penetrating but corrupting intelligence, imperious, jealous of the influence of others; governed by no earnest philosophical or religious belief," having "more elements of anger, however righteous, than of love in his nature."(14)

Although Mazzini rarely mentioned Marx until the period of the International, both Marx and Engels made frequent and often caustic references to Mazzini, regarding him as their arch-rival in the European revolutionary movement. Marx also attacked Mazzini's supporters in England, both British and foreign, especially such figures as George Julian Harney and Ernest Jones and the German exiles Arnold Ruge and Karl Blind, whom Mazzini and Marx saw as possible converts to their respective doctrines. Harney, because of the indiscriminate support he had given to all forms of revolution, was privately referred to by Marx and Engels as "Citizen Hip-hip-hurrah," and Jones, whom Marx considered potentially a most important English convert was sharply criticized for maintaining contact with Mazzini and, through him, with the moderate Chartist factions.(15) Marx was also observant of Mazzini's shortcomings as, for example, when he noted Mazzini's lack of knowledge of economics and his little experience with the Italian people.(16) (The latter view was shared by Herzen who wrote that Mazzini understood only the "cultured" classes of Italy and remained ignorant of the "masses."(17)) Marx later would reiterate his opinion that Mazzini and his followers know nothing of the economic life of the people and, underscoring a major philosophical difference between himself and Mazzini, added that because Mazzini and his supporters were ignorant of the "real conditions of historical moment" they were totally unprepared to participate in revolution.(18)

At other times, however, Marx acknowledged the leading role that Mazzini had played in the European revolutionary movement. In 1853, for example, he observed that, because the Italians had no other alternatives, Mazzini's theory of the legitimacy of assassination as a political weapon was justified.(19) Marx noted of course that it would be actually economic conditions and not individual actions that would precipitate a revolution, but he lauded Mazzini's "morality" for defending his "theory of the dagger" in the English press.(20) He even commended Mazzini for his accuracy in estimating financial conditions in France under the Second Empire, and somewhat in contradiction to previous observations, expressed his hope that Mazzini, the "ablest exponent of the national aspirations of his countrymen," would not stop there, but would continue "to reform his political catechism by the light of economic science." (21) But these public statements belied the actual struggle that was taking place between Mazzini and Marx and Engels. To Marx, Mazzini remained irreconcilably anti-socialist and solidly on the side of the middle classes. Moreover, when the remaining Chartist and emigre factions began to form into socialist and non-socialist camps the antagonism between the two became an open conflict, finally culminating in the struggle for control of the First International.

In 1840 a branch of the Paris-based League of the Just, the forerunner of the Communist League, had been founded in London under the respectable name of the German Workers' Educational Society. It was this emigre socialist society that in November 1847 commissioned the writing of the *Communist Manifesto*. Initially the *Manifesto*, which first appeared in English in Harney's *Red Republican* in 1850, went almost unnoticed, until a year later when the *Quarterly Review* reprinted some excerpts. These passages were given as examples of "Revolutionary Literature" with attention drawn especially to the document's "most anarchical doctrines."(22) By this time radical Chartist had formed the Fraternal Democrats while Mazzini had drawn the moderates into his People's International League. In 1850 Mazzini also founded the Central European Democratic Committee with himself, Ledru-Rollin, Ruge, and Albert Darasq as the executive committee. With the People's International League, this organization helped to unify the non-socialist exile community that, by now, had become quite separated from the socialists.

The Fraternal Democrats ended in 1854 and was replaced in 1856 by the International Association whose main English members were Jones, his Chartist colleague James Finlen, and George Jacob Holyoake. Mazzini boycotted this association because of its adherence to socialism but Marx did attend one of the committee meetings chaired by Jones.(23) Marx then decided to have no further contact with the Association because Herzen, whom Marx hated, had also become involved and in fact addressed the Association's first public meeting. However, Marx's interest was renewed when the International Association decided to establish contact with four groups which became affiliates of the International Association: the German Workers' Educational Society, the English Chartists, the Polish Socialists, and a french socialist organization, the Revolutionary Commune. Mazzini's Young Italy remained outside this affiliation but Marx maintained contact through the Democratic Association in Brussels.(24) Although the International Association lasted only until 1859, its significance lay in the fact that it was the first society, with headquarters in London, to attempt a world-wide organization of labor. Many of those who participated in 1864 in the founding of the International and would become its early leaders had first served their apprenticeship in the International Association.

The International Workingmen's Association, or the First International, developed out of the labor revival that had taken place in Britain and France in the early 1860's. In Britain this revival led to the founding of various organizations and journals such as the London Trades Council in 1860 and the *Beehive*, which began in 1861 and was to become the official organ of the International. Among the leaders of the London Trades Council were William Cremer, who would later serve as the first Secretary of the International, and George Howell, a bricklayer who had led the movement for the nine-hour day in 1858. Cremer, by the early 1860's, was already on close terms with Mazzini, while Howell was to write of this period that "Mazzini was know personally to many of us." (25) Also, from its beginning, the *Beehive* reflected ideas similar to Mazzini's, repudiating in 1863, for instance, the British policy of non-intervention in Italian and East European affairs.(26)

The enthusiasm for the Italian cause among the British working classes during this period was due to both the efforts of Mazzini and the popularity of Garibaldi, especially after his 1864 visit. The idea that the British workers had a special responsibility to support the Italian cause had always been Mazzini's, having developed out of his early association with the Chartists and was fostered by followers and associates during the 1850's. Along with the idea that a special bond existed between the British and Italian working classes, was the notion, common to Mazzini's writings, that the British workers could have a definite influence on their nation's foreign policy. These viewpoints were shared by workers' journals such as Jones' *People's Paper*, which had published an appeal from the Genoese the English workers after the failed uprisings of 1856, and the *Bricklayers' Trade Circular* which wrote in support of Italy's liberation form Austrian rule.(28) These same views, that the British working classes had a special relationship to the cause of Italian unity and that these same classes could effect foreign policy, would later be stressed by Mazzini's follower George Odger in his opening address at the first meeting of the International in 1864.(29) And, as was stated, Garibaldi's tour that same year did much to rouse support among the workers and the trade unions for the Italian cause, despite the fact that there were complaints that he was not permitted to have enough contact with the working classes during his visit. Garibaldi had received deputations of workers from Manchester and other cities and met with Mazzini and other leading exiles, but it was alleged that the government had deliberately kept him away from the workers and had allowed the upper and middle classes to monopolize him during his brief stay.(30)

The other international cause espoused by the British workers was that of Poland. After the Polish uprising in 1863 meetings were held in London between the British and French workers which led directly to a joint declaration of solidarity with the cause of Polish independence. In April of that year a delegation of workers arrived from Paris and met with the English Working Men's Garibaldi Committee. It was this delegation which proposed that a congress of Continental and British workmen be held in London in the near future. Correspondence between the French and the British continued and in July five British trade union leaders, including Odger and Cremer, issued a statement calling for a "grand fraternity of peoples."(31) Meanwhile Mazzini's secretary, Luigi Wolff, was in contact with groups in both countries reporting, at the time, to representatives of British workers on the progress of a strike by porcelain workers at Limoges.(32) The growing movement in both countries for the extension of the workers' franchise had already resulted in the formation of the Universal League for the Elevation of the Industrious Classes. This League, founded by the Marquis of Townsend in February 1864, not only supported universal manhood suffrage, but also stressed cooperation with the working classes of other countries.

Besides the support for the Italian and Polish national causes there were other currents of thought in the background of the development of the First International. Among these were British and French Positivism, and French and German Socialism. The French Socialists, especially, derived their ideas from the teachings of Proudhon. The Positivists, who considered themselves to be disciples of Comte, included such men as Edward Beesly, the chairman of the first meeting of the International, and Frederic Harrison, a writer who had a long association with the trade union movement. What the Positivists shared with the labor movement was a common "anti-Establishment" position. They saw the aristocracy, the Church, and certain sections of the government as the "common foe" of both their own creed and the demands of labor. While opposing class conflict, the Positivists were following Comte's dictum that it would be from within the working classes that the new philosophers would find their most energetic allies.(33) The working classes, in turn, were to lead the way to the conversion of the rest of society to Positivist principles.

Although the French Positivists were represented at the early meetings of the International, the majority of the French delegates were followers of Proudhon. They brought to the organization that thinker's syndicalist position which held that the labor union movement must rely on its own strength and develop its own organizations and institutions rather than seek a compromise with the middle classes or try to participate in a parliamentary government. In this sense the followers of Proudhon were closer to the German Socialists in contrast to the followers of Mazzini who endorsed class cooperation. In August the Beehive published a letter from Victor Le Lubez, a French delegate, announcing a meeting to be held in London on September 28, 1864.(34) It was at this meeting that the First International was formally established and that the conflict between Mazzini and Marx for control of the organization began.

The opening address by Beesly at the International's first meeting called for fraternity between the workingmen of Britain and all other countries and for a reform of British foreign policy.(35) His address was followed by Odger's "Address to the Workingmen of France" which, in both tone and content, showed the influence of Mazzini's ideas. It contained no suggestion of socialism or of a radical change in property relationships. Instead, the working classes were to "clear the way for honorable and comprehensive minds" who would lead and legislate for the masses. Odger's discussion of foreign policy in this address included such concepts as "duties," "reason and moral right," and "dignity" of the working classes which would overcome despotism -- all commonplaces in Mazzini's writings.(36) After the addresses it was decided to elect a committee which would draft a program and rules for the new organization. Thirty-two members were elected to the committee at this meeting and another twenty-three were added shortly afterwards. Half the members were British and the rest consisted of French, Germans, Italians, Swiss, and Poles. The committee, known as the General Council, had as its chairman and general secretary Cremer and Odger and included former Chartists and followers of Owen, Blanqui, and Proudhon, as well as those of Mazzini. Because of these divergent political philosophies and the large number of individuals serving on the General Council the task of developing a program and statutes for the International and achieving a consensus was extremely difficult. Therefore at the first meeting of the Council on October 5 1864, a subcommittee, which included Marx, was commissioned to draw up a set of principles for the organization to be presented at the Council's next meeting.(37)

The Italian members of the General Council, Wolff, Domenico Lama, and Giovanni Fontana, were elected to the Council's program subcommittee and immediately set out to prepare a draft of principles. They used as an outline the program of the Italian Working Men's Association, a London-based organization founded by Mazzini on which each of the three served as executive members. The Association's program, which was commonly referred to as the "Brotherly Agreement," was itself directly inspired by the *Duties of Man* and other writings of Mazzini. Among its provisions, the "Brotherly Agreement" posited the development of an association of workers' societies with three special subdivisions dealing with the moral, intellectual, and economic needs of the working classes. It emphasized the establishment of libraries, schools, and cooperatives, and programs of mutual self-help but avoided all mention of wage or labor struggles, or of conflicts with the other classes. Instead it expressed the need for a "bond of reciprocal and brotherly love" and recommended that the workers make their intentions known to the government by "legal" means.(38) On October 12 Wolff presented a resolution to the Council stating that the principles of the International should be based upon "the promotion of the moral, intellectual, and economical progress of the working classes of Europe," with the goal of achieving "unity of purpose and unity of action." (39) He then read out the text of the "Brotherly Agreement" and suggested that it be adopted as the constitution of the International. Meanwhile another draft of a program and rules for the International was submitted to the Council by one of its members, the former Owenite James Weston. This, in turn, was given by the Council for revision to a French delegate, Lubez, who in his revised draft also submitted a version filled with ideas and phrases clearly inspired by Mazzini.(40) The proposals in Lubez's and Wolff's drafts were then referred back to the main committee, and after a few minor alterations, were enthusiastically received by the members and sent to the subcommittee for a last revision. At the October 15 meeting of the subcommittee a final document, incorporating both Wolff's and Lubez's versions, was accepted as its declaration of principles and rules.(41)

When Marx attended his first full meeting of the Council on October 18 he was shocked at the extent to which Mazzini's influence had permeated the International. The General Council, he told Engels, had approved documents "in which Mazzini could be detected everywhere." (42) Marx immediately acted and with the help of his follower George Eccarius, who was also a member of the General Council, succeeded in getting Lubez's draft sent back to subcommittee for revision. Meanwhile Marx undertook the writing of a new address which he then submitted to the General Council on November 1. By that time three more of his supporters, a Swiss Hermann Jung, Frederich Lessner, a German tailor, and Eugene Dupont, a French musical instrument maker, had also joined the Council. In Marx's version the entire preamble was rewritten and the forty articles in the body of the document were reduced to ten. As a sop to Mazzini's supporters, Marx incorporated parts of Wolff's and Lubez's drafts including references to "truth, justice, and morality," and the phrase "no duties without rights and no rights without duties." Before the document was accepted Marx had to make one final concession and agree to delete the phrase "profit mongers" from his text.(43) This was done at the request of the English delegates George Wheeler and William Worley who had hoped to form a merger between the International and the Universal League. With this, Marx's draft was unanimously accepted by the General Council.

Marx's victory was facilitated by the absence of Wolff who after the October 12 meeting had left London for an Italian workers' conference in Naples. As Wolff was the person closest to Mazzini on the Council his absence made Marx's task considerably easier and Mazzini's other supporters did not recognize the fundamental differences between the earlier documents and Marx's version. Mazzini himself had declined to attend personally any of the International's meetings, preferring instead to be represented by his followers from the Italian Working Men's Association.

Marx's address was written in English and, as he hoped that it would serve to unite the British with the European revolutionary movements, was directed primarily at the British working classes. The address included data from Marx's Capital and dealt in part with British economic conditions, but primarily it spoke of political power and the duty of the working classes to take control from the state.(44) The trade union movement was to play a subordinate role in this process. In the section on foreign affairs, Marx stayed close to the theme of Odger in his earlier address, with one important exception. Marx, like Odger, spoke of the rules of "morality and justice" which governed the relations between nations. But Marx made no mention in this context, as did Odger in his speech, of the "achievements of the Italian liberators" and their struggle for both nationalism and the cause of the workers.(45) Besides having mixed feelings about the Italian national movement, which was not as clearly divided into left and right factions as were other movements, Marx did not want to encourage "the old Mazzinism of Odger, Howell, Cremer, etc."(46)

Mazzini tried to fight back and conceded defeat only grudgingly. On December 13 the 350 members of the Italian Working Men's Association joined the International en masse at Mazzini's instructions, and at the same time issued a manifesto extolling the virtues of their founder's social principles.(47) Marx's statements on morality, justice, rights, and duties which followed the preamble of the address made it possible for Mazzini's followers to stay in the International, and the Italian Working Men's Association along with the London Germans, became its first affiliate. The Italians, following Mazzini, wanted to promote "equal duties and rights for all," along with "true national education," and consumers' and producers' cooperatives.(48) The Germans, on the other hand, stressed the fraternity between "Socialists and Chartists" and explicitly attacked "the rule of the capitalists."(49)

To the Germans and many of the French Mazzini was a reactionary. To the English, however, he remained a hero. A minor incident occurred which was indicative of this division. The English, led by Howell, had proposed a subscription in honor of Mazzini which was vehemently opposed by the German delegates and subsequently had to be dropped. Because of this, Lubez, a supporter of Mazzini, was determined to undermine the German influence on the Council and pressured Marx to replace Eccarius, who was the editor of the International's new organ *Commonwealth*, with Cremer. Marx consented, believing that it was more important to maintain good relations with the English, but also convinced that Mazzini's influence on the Council had to be removed.(50) These divisions were further underscored by a second controversy involving the International's press agent in Paris, Henri Lefort, which was to result in the final resignation of Mazzini's leading supporters from the organization.

The French members of the International had themselves been divided into two groups: the radical republicans, like Lefort and Lubez, who stood for the overthrow of the Empire and the restoration of parliamentary democracy, and the followers of Proudhon who wished to establish a workers' republic based upon cooperatives. In February 1865 the followers of Proudhon protested that Lefort, a bourgeois, was serving as the International's press agent in Paris. Only workers, they believed, should represent a workers' organization. The General Council sent Lubez to investigate and he reported in favor of Lefort. The Council members, including Marx, were forced to choose, and they decided against Lefort. Lubez and other French members resigned in protest and were joined by Wolff, Lama, and Fontana.(51) Marx believed that Mazzini had remained unreconciled sine the rejection of Wolff's draft and had used the incident as an excuse to take his followers out of the organization.(52) But Mazzini did not formally request his other followers to withdraw. In fact he even advised one to "enter the International," as the English elements were "excellent," but warned him also to be on guard against "the influences which aim at the open antagonism between the working and the middle classes, which harm without achieving the task."(53) Although in 1866 Mazzini's English followers still remained on the General Council, all of the Council's corresponding secretaries, including the secretary for Italy, Cesare Orsini, were socialists and supporters of Marx. In February a debate began in the Council over the response of Jung, now representative for Switzerland, to an article on the subject of nationalities. Jung, following Engels, had argued that a distinction must be made between "nations" and "nationalities." Engels' view was that while Europe contained many nationalities -- the Scots, Bretons, and Poles, for example--they did not in themselves constitute nations.(54) Mazzini, who tended to define national movements more broadly, never made such a distinction. At this moment Wolff reappeared and protested against Jung's response, using the opportunity also to reassert Mazzini's position both on nationalism and socialism. Wolff argued that Mazzini's social ideas were especially appropriate for Italy where there were few socialists and no real socialist movement.(55) Marx at this point produced Orsini who stated that Mazzini's teachings had in fact been rejected by the European socialists.(56) Marx's tactics worked and the English withdrew their objections to Jung. In response, Mazzini's Italian followers resigned from the International for a second and final time. "Things are moving," Marx told Engels, "in the next revolution, which is perhaps nearer than it appears, we (you and I) will have this powerful engine in our hands. Compare this with the results of Mazzini's etc. operations during the last thirty years! "(57)

After 1867 Mazzini spent much of his time fighting both socialism and the influence of Marx and the International in Italy. For these purposes he organized a new Italian worker's organization and founded a journal, *Roma del Popolo*, in 1869. There, in a series of articles in 1871 entitled "The International: Addressed to the Working Class," he outlined his reasons for his opposition to the International.(58) It was Mazzini's belief that the International should originally have been structured as a federation of national workers' movements since the large and diverse composition of its General Council, as well as the principle of internationalism, had made the organization unwieldy and its goals impractical. Thus the general council, of which Marx was the "moving spirit," because it ignored the national sections, would either end by acting tyrannically or by not acting at all. In fact, it was for these reasons that the disintegration of the British section begun. And, because the International had denied nationality -- "the idea of Country" -- it had actually attacked the concept of progress which itself was dependent on each nation fulfilling its unique and Providentially-ordained mission. Moreover, because the nation represented the ultimate expression of the idea of association, the International, by positing the commune as the highest social unit, had only brought mankind a step backwards. It had distorted the natural order of social development that begins with the family, passes through the stage of the community, or commune, and reaches completion in the nation. Another error of the International was that it tended to nagate, rather that affirm, the very principle which served as guidelines for the working classes. The first such principle, the belief in the existence of God, had been replaced by the

International with the idea of "self-interest." Consequently, the workers were left without either a hope for the future or a concept of the absolute or a principle in which they could ground their belief in morality.(59)

The other principle negated by the International was that of individual property. Property was the result of labor, the mark of man's performance in the physical world just as the development of his ideas represented his manifestation in the moral world.(60) It was also a stimulus to production beyond what was required to attain the barest necessities of life, and for this reason inequality in possessions was justified since a principle of justice stated that each should receive only according to their merits. Thus, if private property were abolished and collective ownership instituted, all incentive would be destroyed and the freedom of individual labor ended. Of course, society had the responsibility to prevent property from being monopolized or accumulated in any other way than by labor. But in handing the administration of collective property over to the state, the majority would be reduced to a new system of wages which would only reproduce all the evils of the old. Collectivism was a regressive idea, characteristic only of the first stages of social development, and therefore the workers, instead of regressing, should strive to gain both education and the franchise and seek cooperation with the middle classes.(61)

Mazzini also saw the International as severely fragmented. "Which International would you follow?," he asked the workers. The International at Paris had proclaimed the omnipotence of the Commune, while a year earlier at Basle and Zurich it had decreed the supremacy of the State. In 1866 the International had demanded that education be taken out of the hands of the State and left to the discretion of the family; this way, all youth would be brought up in societies that included atheists and believers, monarchists and republicans, thereby learning to live together in fraternity and peace. But in 1869, the Socialists at Geneva had rejected this principle and, declaring themselves atheists, asked for the universal teaching of science in place of religion.(62)

But these were not just examples of the organization's fragmentation. They were also, as in the case of the Zurich declaration, examples of how easily a dangerous notion like the "omnipotence of the State" could be incorporated into the International's program. The inconsistencies in the International's programs were due to the fact that it lacked a systematic and cohesive political philosophy and that its writers and thinkers remained isolated from the people who were told only to contribute, recruit and wait. In fact, the International for all its promises, had done little for the workers, who instead had won their greatest victory of the 1860's -- the extension of the franchise in Britain -- through a league founded solely for that purpose. In contrast, the International, because it lacked focus and specificity and tried to solve all the problems of the worlds's working classes, was doomed to frustration and failure.(63)

In September 1871, in a second series of articles entitled "The International: Part II," Mazzini traced the organization's origin, beginning with the events which had led to its founding in 1864. Here he noted that, because Marx had incorporated so many ideas and phrases which were originally Mazzini's into his Inaugural Address, he felt obliged to the readers of his critique to disassociate himself from both the International's founding and the writing of that address.(64) Mazzini then reasserted his view that the General Council for the beginning had been under Marx's domination and that the International had so exclusively concentrated on the issues of the working class that it had isolated itself from the other important political developments of the time. Moreover, the International's preoccupation with purely economic questions had led to the introduction of the "fatal element" of Communism at its Lausanne conference in 1867. At that time the idea of collectivization was put forth, closing the first stage of the organization's development. The second phase, in which Communism finally triumphed, began in 1868 at the Brussels Congress where it was ruled that all land and utilities should be collectivized and all private property abolished. While in the first stage the International had only made a tactical error and separated economic from political questions, in the second stage it had actually negated "every permanent element of social life" by embracing the collectivist principle.(65) During this latter stage the heights of irrationality and intolerance were reached, as was exemplified by a declaration made at the Basle conference that "if our revolutionary aspirations are in contradiction to science, so much the worse for science."(66)

Mazzini also reiterated his belief in the right of the working classes to education and, noted the plight of those industrial and agricultural workers who, because of their low wages, had to send their children to work just to earn an sustenance for their families. He argued for an increase in salaries for these workers and the shortening of work hours, as well as the exemption of "the necessities of life" from taxation, so that the children would have some years free for schooling instead of having to work to supplement the family income.(67) This stood in contrast to Marx who in general supported child labor and, in 1867, has specifically opposed a resolution in the General Council against that practice arguing that it was a "sound and legitimate tendency."(68) Mazzini asserted that his own economic ideas, which included co-operation between capital and labor, the extension of credit to the workers, the creation of a National Fund, and the cultivation of waste land, were far superior to anything that the International had put forth, and were in fact being co-opted by members of that organization who presented them as their own.(69) In linking the political with the economic in his own program Mazzini believed that he had developed a system that could address three basic errors which he believed were current in the revolutionary thought of the period. The first of these errors was the belief that there existed an infallible political philosophy which, to the exclusion of all others, constituted the ultimate answer to the question of human progress. Communism, especially as represented in the teachings of Marx, was such a system and for this reason would be the most difficult to combat. The second error, that the purpose of revolution was not to continue human progress but to create humanity anew, was also basic to Marx's writings.(70) Because both of these errors failed to take into account the concepts of individuality and liberty, they ultimately would lead to the surrender of control and leadership of the revolutionary process to the state and reintroduce tyranny or worse. The third error, "the vulgarest and most superficial," was the tendency of revolutionary movements to confound temporary and transitory social conditions with the basic conditions themselves. Thus, tyrannical actions were confused with the idea of government, or particular conditions of exploitation with the entire economic system. This error led to anarchism, and because it was based purely on negation rendered society powerless to establish a new order of things over the old.(71)

Mazzini deliberately addressed the issue of anarchism because by 1871 that movement's chief exponent, Michael Bakunin, had become another important rival in the struggle for control of the Italian workers movement. It would be one of Mazzini's last and bitterest conflicts. Mazzini had corresponded with Bakunin as early as 1845, but they only first met during Bakunin's visit to London in 1862.(72) At this time Mazzini was the leading figure in the exile community. Bakunin saw him very often and the two liked and respected each other -- a common bond being their ardent nationalism and mutual hatred of Austria. "The hatred of the Slavs for Germans," Bakunin wrote, corresponds exactly to the hatred of Italy for Austria."(73) For his part, Mazzini supplied Bakunin with letters of introduction to contacts in Italy, and

Bakunin's frequent meetings with Mazzini suggest that he already was considering Italy as a base for revolutionary activity.(74) At this time Bakunin chose not the emphasize any ideological differences he might have had with Mazzini, who, in turn, probably saw Bakunin as a potential political ally or even a possible convert to his ideas. The fact that they shared a common Romantic heritage may also have been a basis of affinity.

However, during his exile in Paris in 1848 Bakunin also had met Marx and was reintroduced to him in London by Marx's disciple Frederich Lessner in 1864. Marx was impressed by what he considered to be Bakunin's abandonment of nationalism for socialism and urged him to support the International and work against Mazzini's republican movement.(75) Mazzini's prestige was still high in Italy, where his moderate position on social issues allowed him to maintain a broad basis of support among the middle classes. But this moderation and tendency to relegate social questions to a secondary level also caused a growing discontent with Mazzini's own republican party. Bakunin, shortly after his arrival in Italy became acquainted with this left-wing republican faction which subsequently published five of his articles in its organ Popolo d'Italia in September 1865. The first article dealt with the issues of atheism and the role of labor in society -- both of which had been a source of contention among Mazzini's followers. Religion, a pillar of the moderates' ideology, was according to Bakunin, a dangerous illusion that portrayed manual labor as "the curse of Adam" and robbed the working classes of their dignity and self-respect.(76) Following articles dealt with the crisis of democracy in Italy, brought about because the republican party had ignored the workers -- the only "true democrats" -- and their needs.(77) However, because Mazzini was still a powerful and respected figure among the Italian radicals, Bakunin did not denounce or even mention him directly. Mazzini in turn did not respond to Bakunin's implicit accusations, although as a result of the growing dissent the left republicans founded another journal in which they published the full text of Marx's address to the International in 1864.(78) The journal, *Liberta e Lavoro*, was in fact one of several that were founded in Italy in the late 1860's -- the period when many of Mazzini's followers became disillusioned with his program and teachings.

But the radical republican faction did not wish to abandon completely the teachings of Mazzini, especially as it lacked a distinct ideology of its own. One interesting result of this was the attempt, by the republican organ *Il Dovere*, to synthesize the ideas of Hegel and Mazzini. Just as Hegel represented the idea of absolute freedom and Mazzini the spirit of Italian liberty, so also their respective theories could form the basis of two braches -- the scientific and political -- of a single movement.(79) The inherent contradictions in such a union apparently were not obvious to the author of these articles, which however, were not without some merit. The theme was inspired by an 1865 essay, "On Caesarism," in which Mazzini had attacked Hegel's doctrines as an exaltation of force.(80) Mazzini was opposed to the growing influence of German philosophy in Italian universities, in particular the teachings of Hegel at the University of Naples. Equating hegelianism with materialism, Mazzini wrote that "one fine day we will sweep out all that stuff."(81) But the argument made by the republican journals posited that these theories were not, in principle, opposed to each other, and that the seeming incompatibility was due only to Mazzini's misinterpretation of Hegel's idea of freedom.(82)

Another dispute developed between Mazzini and some of his followers over questions of government, especially in southern Italy where Mazzini's principle of centralism had been rejected in favor of the idea of local and regional autonomy. However, Mazzini was still elected to the Italian parliament three times from Sicilian districts in 1865, although the governments's ban prevented him from taking his seat. Further disagreement between the moderate and left-wing republicans was precipitated by the Austrian withdrawal from the Italian region of Veneto in 1866. With the end of the Austrian presence in the peninsula Mazzini's argument that the national unification movement must take precedence over questions of social reform was no longer valid, while the position of Bakunin that the social revolution should not be postponed was now vindicated, or at least to many on the left. It became clear to these republicans that Napoleon III and Bismarck, not Mazzini and Garibaldi, had been responsible for the annexation of the Veneto area. Mazzini, concerned over these developments and over the fact that many of the Italian workers might now go over to Bakunin and the International, founded the Universal Republican Alliance in September 1866. His action marked the beginning of a direct confrontation between himself and Bakunin.

Bakunin's weapon against Mazzini and his republican followers was a pamphlet entitled *La Situazione Italiana* which began clandestine publication in Naples in October 1866.(83) *La Situazione Italiana*, and its sequel, *La Situazione II*, represented the first time that the left republicans openly attacked Mazzini, and while they acknowledged Mazzini's role in the European and Italian revolutionary movements, they did not believe that his followers should lead a united Italy. In fact, because the efforts of the moderates had always been extraneous to the needs of the people, they would be in the least effective position to resolve the many social questions that now confronted the new nation.(84) Moreover, Mazzini's idea that such problems could only be solved gradually had actually forced him into an alliance with the conservatives whom his moderate followers had so closely come to resemble. The moderates were now merely part of the "three secular tyrannies" -- the Church, the centralized state, and social privilege -- that were the main oppressors of the people.(85)

Neither Mazzini nor his followers responded to these attacks, perhaps because Mazzini was then in England and in ill health, or because the pamphlets had been published anonymously making a direct response difficult. In 1867 the left republicans founded their own organization, Liberty and Justice, but it still had an economic and political program which in some ways resembled Mazzini's. It called for the institution of credit banks, a people's militia in place of a standing army, and a directly elected judiciary, was well as universal suffrage and freedom of the press, assembly, and religion, the latter of course being demands common at the time.(86) But the organization's journal also published extracts from Marx and Proudhon and various other articles on socialist themes.(87)

Before Mazzini returned to Italy, Bakunin had left for Geneva and founded, in August 1867, the League of Peace and Freedom. His intention was to bring together "all friends of free democracy."(88) Six thousand attended the opening Congress and signatories of the organization's charter included Bright in England, Garibaldi in Italy, Victor Hugo in France, and Herzen for the Russians in exile. Bakunin and Garibaldi were the main speakers at the opening meeting but Mazzini, in a letter to the Congress, declined to take part, citing the organization's pacifism and cosmopolitanism as counter to his nationalist teachings. Mazzini also took the opportunity to reaffirm his belief in centralism as well as the principle of nationality.(89) It was indicative of the great distrust Mazzini had for both Bakunin and his League that not even the endorsement of respected associates such as Victor Hugo or Pierre Leroux could bring him to approve the League's activities. But Mazzini's English followers, Odger and Cremer, did attend in order to explore the possibility of a union between the League and the International. Bakunin also supported such a union and proposed that the League could represent a special political unit within the International, while the rest of the organization concentrated on social and economic issues.(90) However, when this plan was rejected by the General Council he withdrew from the League and founded the International Alliance for Socialist Democracy in 1868. It was through this organization that he continued the struggle against both Mazzini and Marx.

By 1868 Mazzini and Bakunin had both returned to Italy where Bakunin, in the *Situazione* pamphlets, launched a second major campaign against Mazzini attacking his religious ideas as the chief source of his indifference to social issues. In place of Mazzini's moribund republicanism Bakunin proposed a revolutionary movement based upon "atheism, socialism, and federalism."(91) -- principles that were anathema to Mazzini. Mazzini would later write that federalism was merely "a stage of transition between the primitive dispersion of the peoples and unity" and not a "political principle."(92) But at the time Mazzini, who because of his considerable following was still in a position to challenge both Bakunin and Marx provided he recognized certain changing realities in Italian politics, made not direct response. Instead, from his base in Switzerland, he organized a series of uprisings which has as their aim both the overthrow of the monarchy and an attempt to recapture the leadership of the Italian workers' movement. What finally brought him into open polemics with Bakunin was the controversy over the Paris Commune of 1871.

Mazzini had always hated the idea of class war and as early as November 1870 had advised his Italian followers not to join in the factional struggles taking place within the French republican ranks.(93) But, when the Commune was first established his attitude towards that movement was neutral, although he was highly critical of the their government.(94) However, Mazzini was soon shocked by the events in Paris. In April 1871, in his newly founded organ *Roma del Popolo*, he launched his major attack against the Commune.(95) Mazzini especially criticized the federalist principles of the Paris Communards as detrimental to the concepts of the "nation" and "humanity," but still placed the blame for the founding of the Commune on the Versailles Assembly itself.(96) It had been the Thiers government, as weld as the selfishness and indifference of the French ruling classes, which had caused the civil war situation in France. Mazzini expressed the hope that the Italian working classes, in contrast to their French counterparts, would hold national honor higher than economic self-interest and shun civil strife and class warfare.(97)

In a second article, Mazzini again blamed the Thiers government for conditions in France. However, even though he Praised the courage of the Communards, he still believed that it was the Commune itself, under the influence of the International, which represented the greatest threat to liberty and order.(98) Mazzini was especially opposed to the Commune's "declaration"

which had promulgated local autonomy and had proclaimed the inauguration
of a new political era based upon "Positive and Scientific" principles He again
warned young Italian radicals not in imitate this foreign model for revolution,
admonishing that "the Republic, as it is understood by the Commune is not
ours."(99) The fall of the Commune in June 1871 provoked further responses
from Mazzini in which he again blamed the conditions in France on the
doctrines of materialism and atheism.(100) It was these doctrines, originally
developed during the Enlightenment and disseminated by Saint Simon,
Proudhon, Fourier, and others, that had finally corrupted the French people.
Here Mazzini advised his followers to "set aside France and her false
doctrines," because much of what had been done in that country in the name
of liberty had, if fact, ended in tyranny.(101)

Mazzini's attacks in 1871 on both the Commune and the International
incited responses from several sources, including the Italian left. The socialist
journal *Il Gazzettino Rosa* came out in defense of the Commune while
another, La Favilla, directly challenged Mazzini's basic tenets of duty, religion,
and morality as reactionary principles.(102) Some other journals attempted to
change his mind and bring Mazzini over to the cause of the Commune and the
International. The leftist *L'Uguaglianza* cited Mazzini's "Europe: Its
Conditions and Prospects" and the argument that he had put forth in that 1852
article that the workers had a need to emancipate themselves from the tyranny
of capital.(103) In response, Mazzini's own *L'Unita Italiana* published the same
article in it entirety to show that the left-wing journals had misinterpreted his
writings.(104)

Mazzini's criticisms of the Commune and the International served to
separate him further from Garibaldi. Garibaldi had, in part, taken up the
cause of the International to demonstrate his separation from Mazzini, with
whom he was then carrying on a bitter political dispute. The dispute was not
entirely doctrinal, for it also concerned the methods which each leader
believed should be applied in the cause of Italian unity. It became intensified
after each blamed the other for a failed attempt by Garibaldi's forces to
capture Rome in 1867. At that point Garibaldi repeated his charges that
Mazzini was authoritarian and remote from the people, while Mazzini accused
Garibaldi of being overly ambitious and lacking the ability to lead the Italian
democratic movement.(105)

Moreover, since the late 1860's, there was among the republicans, the
development of a belief in a new "science" or system of thought, which was
broadly defined as "materialism" or "rationalism." It had been inspired by

Darwinism and contained elements of positivism and radicalism. Its main exponents came from the ranks of Garibaldi's followers, whom they acknowledged as the nominal leader of the new movement.(106) In the name of science and liberty, the supporters of this new doctrine questioned traditional religious doctrines and practices and, once the polemics over the Commune and the International began, also criticized Mazzini's views on religion and materialism.(107) In August 1871, with Garibaldi's approval, they convened a congress which had as its objective the unification of the various liberal Italian associations into one organization. Mazzini was invited to attend but declined stating that the views concerning religion and the merits of the Commune and the International held by the rationalists would only further divide the liberal movement to the benefit of its enemies.(108) Thus Mazzini, in his last years, had to contend with a new materialist doctrine that was competing for the loyalty of the younger generation of republicans, as well as with the opposition of his former follower and colleague.

But the sharpest attacks on Mazzini's doctrines and his views on the Commune and the International came from Bakunin. In "Reply of an Internationalist to Giuseppe Mazzini," which appeared in the radical *La Liberte* in August 1871, Bakunin started by acknowledging Mazzini's great role as a revolutionary and praising his sincere and noble character, but went on to say that because he had remained attached to an obsolete idealism, Mazzini had ended up on the side of the reactionaries against the popular masses.(109) In his youth Mazzini originally had been divided between two currents of thought -- the theological and the revolutionary. However, in the course of his struggles, Mazzini had given in to the former and became a reactionary. While his opponents, the materialists, were struggling for human liberty, Mazzini and his idealistic followers had become the exponents of public order. Moreover, in turning his back on the Communards, at the very moment when they were being massacred by the reactionaries, Mazzini had betrayed his own democratic teachings and committed an unpardonable crime. Mazzini could not accept the International as the true liberator of the proletariat because he would have had to give up his own role as "high-priest" and prophet of the workers' movement.(110)

Before Bakunin's "Response" appeared Mazzini had already begun a series of articles in *Roma de Popolo* which were essentially a synthesis of his thought and beliefs of the past forty years. In these, as well as in his later articles on the International, Mazzini used the opportunity to respond to Bakunin's charges which he described as "a systematic apology of civil war applied in the guise of a tonic to the nations."(111) A civil war, such as had occurred in 1871 in France, was justified only when a nation was hindered in the fulfillment of its mission by some internal faction or when fought to uphold a program based on moral law. Bakunin, in defending the Commune, was defending class struggle.(112) Mazzini also pointed out the inherent millenarianism in Bakunin's teachings, but was mistaken when he equated Bakunin's socialism with that of Marx and the International.(113) It is also clear from the amount of space he devoted in other writings at this time directly to the issue of anarchism that Mazzini regarded the Communists and socialists as a much greater threat, while the anarchists represented only one of the "many sects and factions" which were destined soon to disappear.(114) Mazzini was more concerned with the temporary damage such movements might do in confusing the republican youth and thereby delaying the advance of the republican cause.(115)

The final stage of the struggle between Mazzini and Bakunin was marked by Bakunin's major critique, "Mazzini's Political Theology and the International," in which he attacked Mazzini's teachings on duty, morality, nationality, and religion.(116) The great error of Mazzini and all the other critics of the International was that they imagined that organization to be a secret society, without morality and dedicated to the destruction of society itself, while their own organizations, such as Mazzini's Republican Alliance, were "divinely" inspired.(117) As idealists, Mazzini and his followers could not understand the issues which moved the real world and had inspired the International's founders. By their idealism and religiosity they had been blinded to the realities of the working classes, and in his hypocritical statements and writings, especially those regarding the Commune, Mazzini had abandoned the cause of the people and sided with reaction. The materialists, whom Mazzini had condemned because they sought to mitigate the plight of the workers were truly upholding an ideal Mazzini and the followers of his "new religion" had abandoned. Moreover, despite his famous formula of "God and the People," Mazzini, in this religion of "duty" and "morality," had actually relegated the people to a secondary and inferior position. Thus, although he truly loved Italy Mazzini, like the biblical Abraham, was willing to sacrifice both her and her people in the name of his new faith.(118)

Again Mazzini made no direct response to Bakunin's article but observed that Bakunin had published a pamphlet against him. "I am now an apostate, a priest, a reactionist, the abettor of Versailles."(119) He also added that the contest between them had to be fought and that he did not regret having opened it.(120) Mazzini also believed that the problems of the working classes could not be ignored and consequently convened the Congress of Workers at Rome in 1871. Through this Congress he hoped to develop a new strategy that would unify the various labor associations and, as he emphasized in his opening address, keep out the socialists so as not to arouse the fears of the middle classes.(121) In response to Bakunin's criticisms Mazzini advised the workers not to discuss "religious, political, and social doctrines," which would only be divisive, and to avoid "foreign societies" which separate the moral from the economic issues and lead to anarchy or despotism.(122) Bakunin replied to Mazzini in a pamphlet addressed to the Italian workers in which he criticized Mazzini's economic program as naive and reactionary and accused him of having shut out the working classes by identifying the "nation" with the "bourgeoisie."(123) Mazzini, in turn, in *Roma del Popolo*, attacked Bakunin's doctrines of equalization of the classes and the abolition of the state and property inheritance, identifying these also as principles of the International.(124) This provoked a response from Engels who used the opportunity to criticize Bakunin who at that moment he considered to be a more important adversary than Mazzini. Engels noted that Bakunin did not represent the International, and that his "narrow and sectarian" program had always been opposed by the General Council.(125) Mazzini, in a response to Engels, noted the irony in the fact that Engels, a German, served as Secretary of the International for Italy. He then took the opportunity to point out the contradictions in the International's pronouncements and made a final appeal to its members to return to the principles that had been affirmed by his followers in 1864.(126)

Bakunin, in the later months of his polemics with Mazzini, who died in March 1872, made an interesting comparison between Mazzini and Marx.(127) Bakunin, like Mazzini, believed that the conflict between the three had been inevitable, noting that since the systems posited by Mazzini and Marx were authoritarian they would only end in corruption. There was, however, an important distinction. While both men were overbearing and doctrinaire, Mazzini's actions, unlike those of Marx, were not motivated by self-interest. Despite the fact that both had visions of creating a world State, it was the theories of Marx, more than those of Mazzini, which would most likely be used by those wishing to gain personal power. There was another important difference between Mazzini, who wanted Italy to be the leader of civilization, and Marx who assigned the same role to the proletariat. Mazzini was truly devoted to his followers and associates and was always willing to forgive them so long as they remained loyal to his basic ideals. Marx, on the other hand, cared only for himself and would not tolerate even the least slight to his vanity.(128)

Following Mazzini's death Bakunin offered a comparison of his political system with that of Mazzini.(129) After paying tribute to Italy's "prophet," Bakunin explained that whereas he had stood for individual and communal autonomy, atheism and federalism, Mazzini had upheld outdated concepts of nationalism, religion, and government. While Mazzini preached class cooperation, he preached the class struggle and social revolution. The Italy Mazzini had planned would have been no different that it was under the monarchy. But so great was Mazzini's influence that at the same time Bakunin recommended to his followers that they must consider a temporary collaboration with those of Mazzini in the struggle against the Italian state.(130) In this sense Bakunin paid a grudging tribute to the appeal of Mazzini and his republican teachings.

Notes

(1) Gaetano Salvemini, Mazzini, p. 183, citing Mazzini, *Life and Writings*, 3:7 ("Principles of Cosmopolitanism," 1834).

(2) Mazzini, Ibid., 4:345 ("Duties of Man," 1858).

(3) Mazzini, Scritti, 18:77 (letter to Maria Mazzini, October 15, 1841).

(4) Ibid.

(5) Mazzini, *Life and Writings*, 6:98 ("Thoughts Upon Democracy in Europe," 1846).

(6) Ibid., p. 102.

(7) Ibid., p. 118.

(8) Ibid., p. 123.

(9) Ibid., 6:187 ("A Last Word Upon Fourierism and Communism 1847).

(10) Ibid.

(11) Ibid., p. 203.

(12) Ibid, p. 215 ("Europe: Its Conditions and Prospects," 1852).

(13) Ibid.

(14) Mazzini, *Scritti*, 92:308 ("The International: Addressed to the Working Class," 1871).

(15) Karl Marx and Frederick Engels, *Collected Works* (40 vols., New York: International Publishers, 1985), 12:57 (Marx to Engels, April 4, 1851).

(16) Ibid., p. 205 (Marx to Engels, September 13, 1851), and 12:passim.

(17) Alexander Herzen, *My Past and Thoughts* (6 vols., London: J. M. Dent, 1924), 3:271-273.

(18) Marx, *Collected Works*, 15: 114 (Karl Marx, "The Monetary Crisis in Europe," 1856).

(19) Ibid., 12:510-511 (Karl Marx, "Manteuffel's Speech, 1853).

(20) Ibid.

(21) Ibid., 15:486-489 (Karl Marx, "Mazzini and Napoleon," 1858).

(22) "Revolutionary Literature, *Quarterly Review*, November 1851, p. 21.

(23) Marx and Engels, *Collected Works*, 19:100 (Marx to Engels, November, 1856.

(24) Henry Collins and Chimen Abramsky, *Karl Marx and the British Labour Movement* (London: MacMillan, 1965), p. 9.

(25) Ibid., p.15,18 citing Howard Evans, Sir Randal Cremer: *His Life and Work* (London, 1909) p. 41, and George Howell, *Labour Legislation, Labour Movements and Labour Leaders* (London, 1902), p. 140.

(26) *Beehive*, January 31, 1863.

(27) *People's Paper*, September 27, 1856 and Collins and Abramsky, Ibid, p. 19 citing Bricklayers' Trade Circular, October 1861.

(28) Reynold's *Weekly Newspaper*, April '0, 1862 and Bricklayers Trade Circular, October, 1861.

(29) *Beehive*, October 1, 1864.

(30) *Beehive*, April 23, 1864 and Herzen, Past and Thoughts, p. 53.

(31) *Beehive*, July 16, 1864.

(32) Mazzini, *Scritti*, 79:81 (letter to Luigi Wolff, July, 1864).

(33) F. E. Manuel, *The Prophets of Paris* (New York: Harper and Row, 1965), p. 105ff.

(34) *Beehive*, September 28, 1864.

(35) *Beehive*, October 1, 1864.

(36) *Ibid.*, and Mazzini, *Life and Writings* 4:345-passim. ("Duties of Man," 1844).

(37) The General Council Minutes of the First International, 1864-1866 (5 vols., London, 1964), 1:20 (October 5, 1864).

(38) Mazzini, Scritti, 80:156 ("The Brotherly Agreement of the Italian Workingmens' Association, 1864).

(39) General Council Minutes, 1:39-40 (October 12,1864).

(40) Ibid.,p. 376.

(41) Ibid.

(42) L. E. Mins, *Founding of the First International: A Documentary Record* (New York, 1937), pp. 48-49.

(43) James Guillaume, *L'Internationale: Documents et Souvenirs, 1864-1878*, 4 vols. (Paris, 1905) 1:11-20.

(44) Ibid., p. 46-50.

(45) Ibid., and *Beehive*, September 28, 1864.

(46) Marx and Engels, *Collected Works* (Marc to Engels, March 4, 1865).

(47) Nello Rossell i, *Mazzini e Bakunin : dodici anni di movimento operai in Italia (1860-1872)*, (Turin, 1927), pp. 137-138.

(48) General Council Minutes 1:37 (December 13, 1864)

(49) Ibid.

(50) Marx and Engels, *Collected Works* (Marx to Engels, March 24 1865).

(51) Collins and Abramsky, Karl Marx, p. 101.

(52) Ibid., p. 104 citing Marx to Engels, July 14, 1875.

(53) Mazzini, *Scritti*, 17:12 (letter to A. Traini April 26, 1865).

(54) F. Engels, *Commonwealth*, March 31, 1866.

(55) General Council Minutes, March 6, 1866.

(56) Ibid.

(57) Marx and Engels, *Briefweshcel*, 3:405 (Marx to Engels, September 11, 1867).

(58) Mazzini, *Scritti*, 92:306 ("The International: Addressed to the Working Class," 1871).

(59) Ibid.

(60) Ibid. p. 320.

(61) Ibid. p. 326.

(62) Ibid.

(63) Ibid.

(64) Ibid. p. 341 ("The International: Part II," 1871).

(65) Ibid.

(66) Ibid. p. 347.

(67) Ibid.

(68) *The Working Man*, March 1, 1867.

(69) Mazzini, *Scritti*, 92:306ff. ("The International: Part II," 1871).

(70) Ibid.

(71) Ibid.

(72) Mazzini, *Scritti*, 27:258-259 (letter to Giuseppe Lamberti, April 19, 1845).

(73) E. H. Carr, *Michael Bakunin* (New York: Random House, 1961), p. 264.

(74) Mazzini, *Scritti*,71:98-216 (letters to F. Campanella and A. Saffi, 1862).

(75) Max Nettlau, *Michael Bakunin* (Berlin, 1902), pp. 200-203.

(76) *Popolo d'Italia*, September 22, 1865 and see Rosselli, *Mazzini e Bakunin*, p. 149 ff. and T. R. Ravindraathan, "Bakunin and the Italians" (PhD. dissertation, Oxford University, 1978).

(77) *Popolo d'Italia*, October 22, 1865.

(78) *Liberta e Lavoro*, March, 1866.

(79) *11 Dovere*, May 7, 1865.

(80) Ibid., April 13, 1865 and Mazzini, *Scritti*, 82:78-91. ("On Caesarism," 1865).

(81) Ibid.

(82) *Il Dovere*, May 7, 1865.

(83) Max Nettlau, *Bakunin et I' Internationale* (Geneva, 1926), p. 77.

(84) Pier Carlo Maseni, ed. *M. Bakunin: Ritratto dell'Italia borghese (1866-1871)* (Bergamo, 1961), p. 24.

(85) Ibid.

(86) A. Romano, *Storia del movimento socialista in Italia* (3 vols., Milan, 1964), 1:249-250.

(87) Ibid.

(88) E. H. Carr, "The League of Peace and Freedom: an episode in the guest for collective society," *International Affairs*, vol. 14, Nov-Dec. 1835, p. 842.

(89) Mazzini, *Scritti*, 86:79-89 ("Letter to the Congress of the League of Peace and Freedom," 1867).

(90) Carr, *International Affairs*, Ibid.

(91) Nettlau, *Bakunin et l'Internationale*, pp 131-146.

(92) Mazzini, *Scritti*, 92:306 ("The International" Address to Working Class," 1871).

(93) Ibid., 90:130 (letter to Alfonso Giarrizzo, November 21, 1870).

(94) Ibid.

(95) Ibid, 92 : 173-189 ("The French Commune, 1871)

(96) Ibid.

(97) Ibid.

(98) Ibid., p. 198.

(99) Ibid.

(100) Ibid., 267ff. ("The Commune and the Assembly," 1871).

(101) Ibid.

(102) *11 Gazzettino Rosa*, June 12, 1871, *La Favilla*, July 18, 1871, and see also Rosselli, Ibid., p. 250.

(103) *L'Uguaglianza*, August 6, 1872 and see Rosselli, Ibid., pp. 256, 279.

(104) *L'Unita d'Italia*, June, 1871 and see Mazzini, *Life and Writings*, 6:215 ff. ("Europe: Its Conditions and Prospects," 1852).

(105) Rosselli, *Mazzini e Bakunin*, p. 255.

(106) Ibid. pp. 153-155.

(107) Ibid.

(108) Mazzini, *Scritti*, 91:173-176 (letter to the Societa Democratica Mirandolese, 1871).

(109) A. Lehring, *Archives Bakounine* (2 vols., Amsterdam, 1961), 1:1:283-292 (M. Bakunin, "Response of an Internationalist to Giuseppe Mazzini," 1871).

(110) Ibid.

(111) Mazzini, *Scritti*, 92:350-369 ("Moans, Shudders, and Recapitulation," 1871)

(112) Ibid.

(113) Ibid.

(114) Ibid. p. 306 ("The International: Addressed to the Working Class," 1871).

(115) Ibid.

(116) Lehring, *Archives Bakunine*, 1, 1:1 (M. Bakunin, "The Political Theology of Mazzini and the International,"
1871).

(117) Ibid. p. 25.

(118) Ibid.

(119) Mazzini, *Scritti*, 91:166 (letter to Emilie Venturi, August 29, 1871).

(120) Ibid.

(121) Lehring, *Archives Bakounine*, 1:2:325-329 (G. Mazzini, "Address to the Congress of Workers at Rome, 1871).

(122) Ibid.

(123) Ibid., p. 313 (M. Bakunin, "To the Worker Delegates at the Congress of Rome," 1871).

(124) *Roma del Popolo*, November, 1871.

(125) Ibid., December, 1871.

(126) Lehring, *Archives Bakounine*, 1:2:418 (Mazzini to F. Engels, December 5, 1871).

(127) Ibid, 1 : 2: 123 (Bakunin, "Karl Marx", 1871)

(128) Ibid.

(129) Ibid., p. 238 (Bakunin to Celso Ceretti, March 13-27, 1872).

(130) Ibid.

EPILOGUE

It is common among Mazzini's biographers to cite the tributes that had been paid to him by such diverse thinkers as the American social reformer Jane Addams and the philosopher Frederich Nietzsche. Addams, in her memoirs, vividly recalled the sorrow of her father upon hearing of the death of Mazzini, while Nietzsche was recorded by his biographer as saying that "of all fine lives," it was Mazzini's that he most envied. (1) Nietzsche was attracted to Mazzini's role as the tragic hero who had consumed himself in total concentration upon a single idea and purpose and as the "poet" who had successfully combined his ideals with action. What such tributes demonstrate is not only the extent to which Mazzini was personally admired by his contemporaries, but also how much interest his writings and teachings had generated among various individuals of the period. This is noteworthy because, since many of Mazzini's writings were an amalgamation of his ideas and those of other thinkers, they were not original or even profound. What made them appealing was Mazzini's ability to combine these ideas with similar concepts and apply them to specific political situations. In this sense, Mazzini was attempting to fulfill one of his more important political objectives, the integration of "thought and action." Such a synthesis of theory and praxis was also, to Mazzini, one of the chief virtues of the English and one of the reasons why he so much identified with them.

But in certain areas of thought, his development was somewhat limited. A lack of sophistication in economics, for example, prevented Mazzini and his followers from applying the principle of "thought and action" to many questions of social reform and limited his understanding of the economic theories of important contemporaries, such as Mill and Marx. However, this was also due in part to the fact that, to Mazzini, the study of economics and other disciplines was important only in the sense that it advanced some preconceived principle. In his analysis of history, Mazzini again reduced everything to a didactic purpose, and considered research and facts as comparatively unimportant because he believed that a sufficient amount of data had already been accumulated by the scholars. In fact, because he viewed the historian's role to be essentially that of a "prophet of a higher social end,"(2) his studies in history were extremely deductive.

Despite these shortcomings, Mazzini's influence as a political thinker and inspiration for nationalist movements, in Europe and elsewhere, has been considerable. As was noted, the influence in England of his writings on such subjects as utilitarianism, socialism, and class cooperation helped to sustain the arguments of "moral force" Chartism and, after 1848, to counter the influence of the most radical revolutionary emigres, especially the socialists. Additionally, his writings on nationalism played a part in the popularization of the Italian cause among the English. For his part, Mazzini, who had brought to England definite concepts of religion and nationalism, was able during the exile, to modify other ideas that he held concerning social reform and constitutional monarchy. The latter, he conceded, was uniquely suited to both the British history and temperament. Thus, although in 1837 he had predicted a "bloody revolution" which would topple the existent order, by 1863 he had completely revised this view and wrote "I know of a country -- and it is the only one -- where the monarchy always had roots, intertwined with the tendencies, ideas, and historic life of the nation. It is England."(3)

Such a revised opinion about conditions in England, although not uncommon for the time, was in Mazzini's case probably due more to fact that because the English setting of has exile was not so insular he felt comfortable changing certain ideas which he had held at the beginning of the exile. In this sense, Mazzini's association with such figures as Mill and Carlyle helped him, as an outsider, to feel legitimized and allowed him to continue to critique and analyze various political and social developments in England. Later, Mazzini would carry this spirit of compromise over to some of his policies for Italy. At the end of the 1860's, for example, he proposed national subscriptions, a petition with the signatures of millions of Italians, and meetings to put pressure on the government. Not only would these ideas have been impossible to implement thirty years earlier, but they would have been inconsistent with Mazzini's political strategies and doctrines calling for direct and violent revolutionary action.

During his last years and after his death, Mazzini's image as a political thinker and his idealistic teachings would play a part in the further development of political and literary thought in Britain. Arnold Toynbee, for instance, in his "Lectures on the Industrial Revolution" in 1884 proclaimed Mazzini as "the true teacher of our age," and cited the *Duties of Man* as more important than the works of Adam Smith and Carlyle.(4) Such interpretations, while perhaps excessive, were not untypical. Among the early Fabians, Mazzini was quite popular -- his name and ideals often being invoked with authority in their speeches and writings. In fact, it was Mazzini's idealistic and anti-materialist teachings which helped to facilitate the merger of late 19th century British Idealism with Fabian socialist thought.(5) The Fabian Sydney Olivier endorsed Mazzini's writings on materialism and another, William

Clarke, wrote that he had been strongly affected by Mazzini's political religion and the idea that "political questions could not be separated from religious [ones]"(6) Mazzini was also highly regarded by the British Marxist and leader of the Social Democratic Federation, H. M. Hyndman, who although he disagreed with the thinker on several major issues, frequently sought him out during the last years of his exile to discuss questions of nationalism and revolution.(7) Later, the Positivist Frederic Harrison wrote that he himself had been extremely impressed by Mazzini's personality and genius, and acknowledged that he had been one of the main influences in the development of his own political beliefs.(8) Other of Mazzini's contemporaries would recall how he profoundly impressed them with his sincerity and idealism. John Morley, for example, although he deplored Mazzini's disbelief in compromise and his lack of patience, felt that he had stood for "the voice of conscience in modern democracy," and had been "as earnest as Kant himself in urging the moral relations between different States."(9)

What is significant about such comments and reflections on Mazzini is the extent to which they reveal the diversity of his appeal. Each of these thinkers held views widely divergent from each other and from Mazzini, yet each paid him tribute and acknowledged him as a source of personal, if not political, inspiration. This was due to the fact that, like others, they were drawn more to his spirit and person than to his ideas and principles and were inspired by his idealism and his image as a leading revolutionary figure of the age. As had been the case throughout his exile, Mazzini's charismatic personality had transcended whatever political differences he might have had with his many admirers.

The appeal which Mazzini and his ideals had for the British is also evident in literary works of the period. George Meredith, who had read proof for the collected edition of Mazzini's works, modeled the central character of his serialized novel, *Vittoria* (1864-1865) on Mazzini.(10) The novel, which ran in The *Fortnightly Review*, in many ways represents the high point of Mazzini's influence on English letters. Set in 1848, Meredith's work describes Mazzini at the height of his romantic revolutionary career, and speaks of its protagonist, the "Chief," with his "dark, meditative eyes," full of "contemplative energy," his visage in which "the passions were absolutely in harmony with the intelligence," and his abhorence of "present material interests."(11) Later, Disraeli, in his novel *Lothair* (1870), did much the same, presenting Mazzini under the guise of the character "Mirandola," but emphasizing the political disappointments of his later years as well as his early idealism.(12) An accurate and insightful portrait of Mazzini in his last period of exile, the novel describes the maladies which beset him at that time and his disillusionment with what he believed to be the materialism of many of his supporters. Characteristically, "Mirandola" plans to issue a manifesto "addressed to the peoples," exhorting them to fulfill their duties towards the family, the nation, and humanity, and to obey God's moral law.(13)

Mazzini's influence on English letters is evident too in the works of several of his British followers, including his translator and his biographer, Jessie White Mario and Emilie Ashurst Venturi, each of whom had married one of his compatriots. Mario, who had taken part in the attempted republican coup at Genoa in 1856, would, in 1909, be the author of a history of modern Italy,(14) while Venturi, whose family had been among Mazzini's closest British friends and supporters, later became one of his earliest biographers.(15) Both typified the intense devotion which Mazzini inspired among many of his female followers and served as the inspiration for at least one novel. *Clara Hopgood* (1896), by William Hale White, details Mazzini's life during his early exile, including his dealings with the Chartists, and ends with its heroine -- unlike any of Mazzini's actual English disciples -- dying for the cause of freedom in Italy.(16)

Mazzini was the subject of some of the poetry of the period, including works by the Brownings and A. C. Swinburne. In fact, Mazzini appeared quite early in some of these poems, such as Robert Browning's "The Italian in England," (1845) which Browning wrote in response to accusations made against Mazzini during the Post Office Espionage case. Later, Mazzini was be the subject of Swinburne's panegyric, "Ode to Mazzini" (1857), in which the exile returns victoriously to his liberated homeland, and in "Super Flumina Babylonis"(1869), in which Swinburne portrays Mazzini as the prophet who would inspire the Italians to rise and escape their own "Babyonian exile."(17) Of course, Mazzini figured in the memoirs and recollections of many prominent British leaders of the period, such as Gladstone and Palmerston, and in those of old associates like Carlyle and several of the radicals and Chartists. In the latter works he was especially recalled with a sense of affection and respect and a recognition of his effect upon British thought.

However, it was ultimately in Italy where Mazzini's image, influence, and teachings would have the widest application and effect. Paradoxically, in the period immediately after unification, many of his Italian followers found his ideas to be irrelevant to the new nation. His disciple Francesco Crispi, for instance, who became Prime Minister in 1887, had like others rejected

Mazzini's republican program in favor of a more pragmatic system under the monarchy. But in the last decade of the century, when disillusionment with post-unification governments had set in, Mazzini's writings again seemed applicable. To the next generation of republicans it seemed that Mazzini's predictions concerning the inabilities of the monarchist government to resolve problems of education and social reform had been accurate. At the same time, other of Mazzini's theories were co-opted by Italian expansionists who, claiming inspiration from the Risorgimento, identified Mazzini's idea of the "leadership of Rome" with domination abroad and his concept of the "mission of Italy" with colonial conquest. For nationalists such as the writer Alfredo Oriani, expansion was a national duty and he used the ideas of Mazzini in combination with the writings of Italian Hegelians to develop a rationale for the establishment of the colonial empire.(18) After 1911 Mazzini's writings on the "national mission of Italy were used by other irredentists to justify Italy's claims for territory in Europe as well as in Africa and the Middle East. With the beginning of the First World War, many of these nationalists employed Mazzini's theories to reinforce a policy of intervention calling for an alliance of the Italians and Slavs against Austria and Germany. "Mazzini in 1871 prophesied the alliance of Italy with the Slavs," prime Minister V. E. Orlando explained in 1917, "we are today fulfilling that prophesy."(19)

After the war many historians saw in Woodrow Wilson's peace plan the realization of Mazzini's ideas. Mazzini, for example, had proposed the formation of an international organization, similar to the League of Nations, which was to uphold the ideals of peace, national sovereignty, and self-determination. In many respects the map of Europe as it was redrawn after the Treaty of Versailles resembled Mazzini's plans for new ethnic and national boundaries. In 1922, David Lloyd George noted "how right" Mazzini had been about European affairs.(20)

At the same time, however, Mazzini's ideas and teachings were being applied by Benito Mussolini and other fascist thinkers to their policies and programs. Mazzini's idealism and his preoccupation with nationalism, duty, and self-sacrifice, as well as his emphasis on political activism, easily lent themselves to the rhetoric of the Fascist Party. His "Thought and Action" doctrine, for instance, which had been conceived as an appeal to the intellectuals and thinkers of his day to put their beliefs into practice, was change by Mussolini's Minister of Education, Giovanni Gentile, into an anti-intellectualist manifesto glorifying fascism. It was Mussolini, the philosopher Gentile wrote, who gave "the most rigorous meaning to Mazzini's maxim of 'thought and action.'"(21) In his own program of educational reform, Gentile employed Mazzini's teaching on that subject to purge the Italian schools of what was perceived to be a narrow and positivistically inspired intellectualism.

Mazzini's emphasis on youth and idealism also proved useful to the fascists. The writers of the fascist journal *Ottobre*, recalling that nearly a century before Mazzini had organized Young Europe, in 1930 called for the establishment of a new Young Europe movement that was to serve as the basis for an international fascist organization. "We conceive of the Fascist International according to the teachings of Mazzini: 'Like a militant Church with a task to achieve. '"(22) In 1933, such a body, the Action Committee for Roman Universality, was actually established. It combined Mazzini's emphasis on youth and international organization with his theory that Italy, under the direction of Rome, was to lead in the regeneration of western civilization.

If Mazzini's teachings were easily co-opted by the fascists, they were also employed by the Italian anti-fascists, albeit with less success. Mazzini's republicanism was used by the resistance as a rallying cry against both fascism and the Savoy dynasty which had allowed Mussolini to come to power. Several partisan units were named "Mazzini Brigades" and in 1939 emigre Italian anti-fascists, led by Gaetano Salvemini, founded the Mazzini Society. Its purposes were to help in the coordination of the resistance movement abroad and to promote the idea of a post-war republican government in Italy. The Society, whose membership never exceeded 2,000, sought to represent the principles of Mazzini in the title of its organ, United Nations, and in such policies as the exclusion of Communists from its roster.(23) (This policy, however, did not preclude collaboration with the Italian Communist Party for the duration of the war.)

The Italian Republican Party and others, like the Radicals, also traced their origins to Mazzini and his Action Party, but for many years they were overshadowed by the monarchists and later would be banned under fascism. Although during World War I the Republicans joined the nationalists and in the name of Mazzini called for Italian intervention on the side of the Allies, they had greater difficulty in reconciling Mazzini's teachings to their domestic policy. This was because the Republicans faced the dilemma of trying to integrate Mazzini's centralist position with the federalist policies of the Italian state. Many, in fact, opted to follow the federalism of other 19th century republicans and nationalists such as Carlo Cattaneo. With the proclamation of the Italian republic in 1946, it seemed to many historians and political writers that Mazzini and his teachings would finally triumph. It soon became clear, however, that some of these, such as his theories on centralism, would be inapplicable or impossible to implement. Also, his political theology, based on the concept of "God and the People," was rejected by the new republic in favor of Cavour's formula of "a free Church in a free state." This fact is significant because the concept of a "Church of the People" was one of the cornerstones of Mazzini's teachings. Mazzini had thought that the idea of the separation of Church and state was absurd and that if it were achieved the moralizing effect of religion on society would be lost. He was unable to see that the separation envisioned by Cavour did not preclude this influence. In fact, this separation could be interpreted as favoring religion by freeing it from political entanglements and commitments. In reality, of course, this policy has not been evenly applied in post-war Italy, but that does not negate the efficacy of the principle.

Other of Mazzini's ideas and writings are relevant today especially those critical of other ideologies. Among his works which can be read with profit are those on utilitarianism, socialism, and communism, including "Thoughts Upon Democracy in Europe" and the series of articles on the First International. In both of these he correctly identified the inherently illiberal nature of these ideologies and their tendency to reduce society to the level of "bees" and man to a "cypher."(24) He stressed the potential for despotism latent in systems that denied incentive and the right to private property and noted that because such systems are a priori anti-religious they must ground morality in a materialistic principle like the state and become even more repressive and rigid. Mazzini correctly saw Bentham's utilitarianism as the inspiration for such subsequent despotic systems and was also correct in his prediction that they would be rejected by the British working classes. Mazzini understood that liberty was the one principle antithetical to Bentham's schema for a new society based upon the principle of "the greatest happiness for the greatest number." Such a system could not tolerate the freedoms of personal choice or dissent.

Additionally, Mazzini's literary analyses of various thinkers and their works, such as his essays Carlyle, are noteworthy, especially for their style and the perceptive critique Mazzini gave of his subjects.(25) And, although his biographer Bolton King had overstated the case in affirming that Mazzini could have been among the greatest literary critics of his age(26), Mazzini's extensive literary works, including Sarpi, Hugo, George Sand, and Byron and Goethe can be considered useful commentaries on 19th century literature.(27)

Other of Mazzini's writings, however, especially on subjects like nationalism and political action must, in light of the events of modern history, be read more critically. While such concepts as duty, morality, and self-sacrifice are, in themselves, worthy themes, the misuse and misapplication of Mazzini's teachings on these subjects have demonstrated just how problematic these terms are for our times. Other of his teachings on subjects like tyrannicide are even more tenuous and difficult to justify, for they too have been easily adapted to the rhetoric and policy of authoritarian and totalitarian regimes. In the end, such writings must be understood in the context of Mazzini's idealism and limited political experience, as well as his romantic and revolutionary heritage.

Notes

(1) Ignazio Silone, *The Living Thoughts of Mazzini* (London: Cassell and Co., 1939)), citing Jane Addams, *Forty Years at Hull House* (New York, 1919), p. 21, and Malwida von Meysenbug, *Der Lebensabend einer Idealisten* (Berlin, 1905), p. 90, and see also Barr, Griffith, King, and Salvemini.

(2) Mazzini, *Life and Writings*, 4:209 ("Duties of Man," 1844).

(3) Mazzini, *Scritti*, 75:142 ("The Monarchies and Us," 1863).

(4) Alon Kadish, *Apostle Arnold, the Life and Death of Arnold Tovnbee* (Duke University Press, 1986), p. 109 and p. 2 citing *Bradford Chronicles*, February 1, 1881.

(5) Willard Wolfe, *From Radicalism to Socialism* (New Haven: Yale University Press, 1975), p. 274.

(6) Ibid., p. 241.

(7) Chishichu Tsuzuki, *H. M. Hyndman and British Socialism* (London: Oxford University Press, 1961), p. 11.

(8) Frederic Harrison, *Autobiographical Memoirs* (London, 1911). pp. 97-99.

(9) John Morley, *Recollections* (London, 1917). pp. 78-79.

(10) George Meredith, *Vittoria* (London, 1909), pp. 9-10.

(11) Ibid.

(12) Benjamin Disraeli, *Lothair* (London, 1881), pp. 164-168 and see H. W. Rudman, *Italian Nationalism and English Letters*, pp. 153-154.

(13) Ibid.

118

(14) Jesse White Mario, *The Birth of Modern Italy* (London, 1909).

(15) Emilie Ashurst Venturi, *Mazzini: a Memoir* (London, 1875).

(16) William Hale White [Mark Rutherford], *Clara Hopgood* (London, 1896).

(17) Edmund Gosse, *The Life of Algernon Swinburne* (London, 1930), and Edmund Gosse and Thomas James Wise, eds., *The Complete Works of Algernon Charles Swinburne* (London, 1925), p. 153.

(18) A. Oriani, *Fino a Dogali* (Bologna, 1923), pp. 82-83, 152-156.

(19) S. Cilibrizzi, *Storia elamentare, politica e diplomatica d'Italia,* 7:342 (8 vols., Naples, 1939-1952), and see C. Seton-Watson, *Italy from Liberalism to Fascism 1870-1925* (London: Methuen, 1967), p. 495.

(20) E. E. Y. Hales, *Mazzini and the Secret Societies* (New York: P. J. Kenedy, 1956), p. 202.

(21) Adrian Lyttelton, ed. *Italian Fascisms From Pareto to Gentile* (New York: Harper and Row, 1975), p. 302 citing G. Gentile, "The Origins and Doctrine of Fascism," 1934).

(22) *Ottobre*, July 16, 1933.

(23) Charles F. Delzell, *Mussolini's Enemies: The Italian Anti-Fascist Resistance* (Princeton: University Press, 1961), pp. 201-209.

(24) Mazzini, *Life and Writings,* 6:103 ("Thoughts Upon Democracy in Europe,: 1846).

(25) Mazzini, *Life and Writings,* 4:56-109 ("On the Genius and Tendency of the Writings of Thomas Carlyle," 1843), and pp. 110-144 ("On the History of the French Revolution, by Thomas Carlyle," 1843).

(26) Bolton King, *The Life of Mazzini* (New York, 1909), p. 312.

(27) see Mazzini, *Life and Writings*, 2:221-256 ("Paolo Sarpi," 1838), 257-302 ("On the Poems of Victor Hugo," 1838), and 6:33-60 ("George Sand," 1839), and 61-97 ("Byron and Goethe," 1839).

SELECTED BIBLIOGRAPHY

Primary Sources:

Major primary sources include the vast collection of Mazzini's writings, the 98 volumes of the *Scritti editi ed inediti* (1905-1973), containing almost all his correspondence and writings in English and Italian, and the 6 volume series in English, *Life and Writings of Joseph Mazzini* (1862). The latter is useful as it includes translations of such important works as Mazzini's "Autobiographical Notes" and many of his earlier essays and articles.

Alden, W. L. "Mazzini's Last Manifesto," *The Galaxy*, March 1867, pp. 484-492.

Bagehot, Walter. *Historical Essays*. Edited by N. St. John-Stevas. Garden City: Doubleday, 1965.

Bianchi, Nicomede. *Storia documentata della diplomazia in Italia dall' anno 1814 all' anno 1861*. 8 vols. Turin: 1872.

Blind, Matilde. "Personal Recollections of Mazzini, *The Fortnightly Review*, May 1891, pp. 702-718.

Buckle, T. H. "Mill on Liberty," *Frazer's Magazine*, vol. 59, 1859, pp. 509-542.

Carlyle, Thomas. *The Centenary Edition of the Works of Thomas Carlyle*, 30 vols. Edited by H. D. Traill. London: Chapman and Hall, 1896-1899.

Letters and Memorials of Jane Welsh Carlyle. Edited by James A. Froude. New York: Scribner's, 1883.

Castelar, Emilio. "The Republican Movement in Europe," *Harper's New Monthly Magazine*, New York, vol. 45, 1872.

Cilibrizzi, S. *Storia parliamentre, politica e diplomatica d'Italia*, 8 vols. Naples: 1839-1952.

Comte, Auguste. *The Positive Philosophy*. Translated by Harriet Martineau. London: John Chapman, 1853.

Conway, Moncure D. *Autobiography: Memoirs and Experiences*. 2 vols. London: Chapman and Hall, 1904.

Documents of the First International: The General Council Minutes 1864-1872. 5 vols. Moscow-London, 1964.

Duncombe, Thomas S., M.p. *The Life and Correspondence of Thomas S. Duncombe*, M.P. 2 vols. London: Hurst and Blackett, 1868.

Engels, Frederich. *The Condition of the Working Class in England*. Translated by W. O. Henderson and W. H. Chaloner. London, 1958.

Fourier, F. C. M. *Ouevres Completes*. 6 vols. Paris: Calmann, 1846-1848.

Froude, James A. *Thomas Carlyle, A History of his Life in London 1834-1881*. London: Longmans, Green and Co., 1897.

Garibaldi, Giuseppe. *Autobiography*. 3 vols. London: Walter Smith and Innes, 1889.

Garrison, William Lloyd. *Joseph Mazzini. His life, writings and political principles*. New York: Hurd and Houghton, 1872.

Hansard's *Catalogue and Breviate of Parliamentary Papers*. Oxford: Blackwell, 1953.

Harrison, Frederic. *Autobiographic Memoirs*. 2 vols. London: Chatto and Windus, 1911.

Harro-Harring, Paul. *Memoires sur la Jeune Italie et sur les derniers evenements de Savoie*. Paris, 1834.

Hegel, Georg Wilhelm Frederich. *The Philosophy of History*. Translated by J. Sibree. New York: Dover, 1956.

Herzen, Alexander. *Past and Thoughts*, 6 vols. London: Chatto and Windus, 1924.

Holyoake, George Jacob. *Bygones Worth Remembering*. London: J. M. Dent, 1902.

Sixty Years of an Agitator's Life. 2. vols. London: J. M. Dent, 1902.

Howell, George. *Labour Legislation, Labour Movements, and Labour Leaders*. London: Laurence and Buller, 1902.

Kant, Immanuel. *The Philosophy of Kant*. Edited by Carl J. Frederich. New York: Modern Library, 1949.

Jones, E. R. *The Life and Speeches of Joseph Cowen*, M.P. London: Longman's, 1885.

Lehring, A. *Archives Bakounine*. 2 vols. Amsterdam: International Institute for Social History, 1961.

Linton, William James. *European Republicans: Recollections of Mazzini and His Friends*. London: Laurence and Buller, 1892.

"Some European Republicans." *Century Illustrated Monthly Magazine*, April, 1886, pp. 407-411.

Lovett, William. *Life and Struggles*. London: MacGibbon and Kee, 1876.

Magliano, Bice Pareto. "Some First-Hand Recollections of Mazzini," *The Contemporary Review*. November, 1917, 565-72.

Marx, Karl and Engels, Frederich. *Briefweschsel*. 4 vols. Berlin, 1950.

Collected Works 40 vols New York : International Publishers, 1985.

Mazzini, Joseph. *Life and Writings*, 6. vols. London: Smith, Elder and Co., 1892.

Scritti editi ed inediti, 98 vols. Edited by A. Codignola, G. Daelli, E. Morelli, V. E. Orlando, et al. Imola: 1905-1973.

Mill, John Stuart. *Autobiography*. Indianapolis: Bobbs, Merrill, 1957.

Collected Works; 1849-1873. 24 vols. Edited by Francis E. Mineka and Dwight N. Lindley. Toronto: University of Toronto Press, 1972.

The Earliest Letters of John Stuart Mill: 1812-1848. Edited by Francis E. Mineka. Toronto: University of Toronto Press, 1963.

Politics and Culture. Edited by Gertrude Himmelfarb. New York: Anchor, 196,

Mill's Utilitarianism. Edited by J. M. Smith. Belmont: Wadsworth Publishing, 1959.

Bentham and Coleridge. Edited by F. R. Leavis, London: 1962.

The Subjection of Women, and Mill, Harriet Taylor. *The Enfranchisement of Women*. London, 1983.

Milnes, Richard M. *The Events of 1848, Especially in Their Relation to Great Britain*. London, 1849.

Mins, L. E., ed. *The Founding of the First International: A Documentary Record*. New York, 1937.

Morley, John. *Recollections*. 2 vols. London, 1917.

Saint-Simon, Henri, comte de. *Selected Writings*. Edited and translated by F. M. H. Markham. Oxford: Oxford University press, 1952.

Stern, Daniel *Histoire de la Revolution de 1848* London, 1857.

Tocqueville, Alexis. *Tocqueville and Beaumont on Social Reform*. Edited by Seymour Drescher. New York, 1968.

Toynbee, Gertrude. *Reminiscences and Letters of Joseph and Arnold Toynbee*. London, n.d.

Toynbee, Joseph. *Lectures on the Industrial Revolution in England*. London, 1884.

Venturi, Emily Ashurst. *Joseph Mazzini. A Memoir*. London: King Publishers, 1877.

Manuscript Collections:

Aberystwyth. National Library of Wales. William Rees Collection (Correspondence of Mazzini to Rees).

Glasgow. Glasgow University Library. John McAdam Collection (Correspondence of Mazzini to McAdam). 214

Manchester. Cooperative Union, Ltd., Holyoake House. George Jacob Holyoake Collection (Correspondence of Mazzini to Holyoake)

Newcastle-upon-Tyne. Newcastle-upon-Tyne Central Library. Joseph Cowen Collection (Correspondence of McAdam to Cowen).

Journals, Newspapers, and Periodicals British:

Beehive, January 31 1863; April 23, July 16, September 28, October 1 1864.

Bricklayers Trade Circular, October 1861.

British and Foreign Review, October 1848.

Commonwealth, April 16, 1867.

Daily News, July 5, 1855.

Edinburgh Review, June, 1829.

English Republic, 1851-1852.

Fortnightly Review, November 1841.

Friend of the People, 1847-1848.

The Globe, June 6, 1844.

Monthly Chronicle, March 1839, January 1840.

Morning Advertiser, March 23, 1855.

North British Review, March 1844.

Northern Star, 1844-1846.

Notes to the People, 1851-1852.

People's Journal, 1846-1850.

People's Paper, June 8, 1856.

Punch, May 5, 1844.

Quarterly Review, July 1851.

Reasoner, 1850-1852.

Red Republican, 1850-1851.

Reynolds Weekly Newspaper, April 20, 1862.

The Times (London), July 5, 1844; October 5, 1856.

Westminster Review May 1837; January 1842; June, 1843.

The Working Man, April 6, 1867.

Italian:

Apostolato Popolare, 1837-1839.

Il Dovere, June 1859; May 1865.

Liberta e Lavoro, April 1866.

Il Favilla, July 10, 1871.

Ottobre, July 16, 1933.

Popolo d'Italia, September 22, 1865.

Roma del Popolo, 1869-1872.

L'Ugualianza, August 6, 1872.

L'Unita d'Italia, June 1871.

French:

La Liberte, August 1871.

Reference Works:

Acton, Harold. *The Last Bourbons of Naples*, 1825-1861. New York: St. Martin's Press, 1961.

Barbieri, M. "Sul Giacobinismo di Giuseppe Mazzini, 1831." *Risorgimento* 33 (1981): 197-245.

Barrili, A. G. *Con Garibaldi alle e di Roma*. Milan: Treves, 1895.

Barr, Stringfellow. *Mazzini: Portrait of an Exile*. New York: Henry Holt and Co., 1935.

Beales, Derek. *England and Italy, 1859-1860*. London: T. Nelson, 1959.

Berkley, George F. *Italy in the Making, 1815-1846*. Cambridge: Cambridge University Press, 1932.

Italy in the Making, June 1846 to 1 January 1848. Cambridge: Cambridge University Press, 1936.

"The Mental Development of Italian Nationality, 1815-1848," *The Nineteenth Century and After 121* (1937): pp. 91-102.

Berlin, Isaiah. *Karl Marx*. Oxford: Oxford University Press, 1979.

Berta, Giuseppe. Marx, *Gli Operai Inglesi e i Cartisti*. Milan: Feltrinelli Economica, 1979.

Berti, G. "La dottrina Pisacanaina della rivoluzione sociale," *Studi Storici* 1(1) (1959/60): pp. 24-61.

Bondanella, Peter and Julia Conaway. eds., *Dictionary of Italian Literature*. Westport: Greenwood Press, 1979.

Bourgeois, Emile and Clermont, E. *Rome et Napoleon III, 1849-1870*. Paris: Librairie A. Colen, 1907.

Bourne, K. "The British Government and the Proposed Roman Conference of 1867," *Rassegna Storia del Risorgimento* 43 (1956): pp. 759-63.

Bowle, John. *Politics and Opinion in the Nineteenth Century*. London: Jonathan Cape, 1954.

Briggs, Asa, ed. *Chartist Studies*. London: Macmillan, 1965.

Brinton, Crane. *English Political Thought in the Nineteenth Century*. Oxford: Oxford University Press, 1933.

Brock, P. "Polish Democrats and English Radicals, 1830-62," *Journal of Modern History* 25 (1953): pp. 81-97.

Cafagna, L. "Intorno al Rivisionismo Risorgimentale." *Studi Storici* 1 (1959/60) pp. 24-61.

Carr, E. H. *The Romantic Exiles*. London: Macmillan, 1933.

"The League of Peace and Freedom: an episode in the quest for collective security," *International Affairs* 14 (1935), pp. 839-851.

Michael Bakunin. New York: Macmillan, 1937.

Caute, David. *The Left in Europe Since 1789*. New York: McGraw Hill, 1971.

Codignola, Arturo. *Mazzini*. Turin: Einuardi, 1946.

Cofer, D. B. *Saint-Simonism in the Radicalism of Thomas Carlyle*. Austin: Von Boeckmann-Jones, 1931.

Cole, G. D. H. Chartist Portraits. New York: Macmillan, 1965. and Filson, A. W. *British Working Class Movements Select Documents - 1789-1875*. London: Macmillan, 1950.

Collins, H. and Abramsky, C. *Karl Marx and the British Labour Movement*. London: Macmillan and Co., 1965.

Colombo, A. "Un inedito di Bakunin sul morte di Mazzini, 12 maggio 1872." *Annali di Istituto G. Feltrinelli* 14 (1974) pp. 174-183.

Coppa, Frank J. "The Religious Basis of Giuseppe Mazzini's Political Thought." *Journal of Church and State* 12 (1970): pp. 237-253.

____ *Camillo di Cavour*. New York, Twayne Publishers, 1973.

130

___ *Pope Pius IX*. Boston: Twayne Publishers, 1979.

___ ed. *The Dictionary of Modern Italian History*. *Westport: Greenwood Press, 1983.*

Cowling, Maurice. *Mill and Liberalism*. Cambridge: Cambridge University Press, 1963.

Crane, Walter. *An Artist's Reminiscences*. London, 1907.

D'Alessandro, A. "La republica romana deI 1849 e l'intervento francese," *Nuovo Rivista Storica* 41 (1957): pp. 261-289.

Dale. R. W. "George Dawson: Politician, Lecturer, and Preacher." *Nineteenth Century*, July, 1877, pp. 45-56.

Dawson, W.H. *Richard Cobden and Foreign Policy*. London: Routledge and Keagan Paul, 1927.

Della Peruta, Franco. "La Revolution Frangcaise dans pensee des Democrates Italiens du Risorgimento," *Annales Hist. de la Revolution Francaise 49* (1974): pp. 664-676.

Delzell, Charles F. Mussolini's Enemies: *The Italian Anti-Fascist Resistance*. Princeton: University Press, 1961.

DeSanctis, F. *Mazzini*. Bari: Laterza, 1920.

Deiss, Joseph J. *The Roman Years of Margaret Fuller*. New York: Thomas Y. Crowell, 1969.

Duncan, William. *Life of Joseph Cowen*. Newcastle-upon-Tyne: W. Scott, 1904.

Ericksen, Arvel. *The Public Career of Sir James Graham*. Oxford: Oxford University Press, 1952.

Evans, Howard. *Sir Randal Cremer: His Life and Work*. London, 1906.

Fisher, H. A. L. *The Republican Tradition in Europe*. London, 1911.

Galimberti, A. "Mazzini nel pensiero inglese." *Nuova Antologia* 7 (1919): pp. 17-24.

Gallavresi G. "British Friends of the Italian Risorgimento." *Contemporary Review*, September, 1929.

Gash, N. *Politics in the Age of Peel*. London: Oxford University Press, 1952.

Garrone, A. "L'Emigrazione politica italiana deI Risorgimento." *Rassegna Storica deI Risorgimento* 41 (1954): pp. 223-242.

Filippo Buonarroti e i rivoluzione dell'Ottocento, 1827-37. Florence: Einuardi, 1951.

Gentile, G. *I profeti deI Risorgimento Italiano*. Turin: Einuardi, 1924.

Ghisalberti, Alberto M. *Momenti e figure deI Risorgimento Romano*. Milan: A. Giuffre, 1965.

Roma da Mazzini a Pio IX. Ricerca sulla restaurazione papale deI 1849-50. Milan: A. Giuffre, 1958.

Gossman, Norbert J. "Republicanism in Nineteenth Century Italy," *International Review of Social History* 7 (1962): pp. 117-131.

Griffith, Gwilym, *Mazzini Prophet of Modern Europe*. New York: Howard Fertig, 1932

Grugel, Lee. *George Jacob Holyoake,a study in the evolution of a Victorian radical*. Philadelphia: Porcupine Press, 1976.

Guardione, F. "Confessioni postume inglesi sulla violata corrispondenza dei Bandiera col Mazzini, *Rassegna storica deI Risorgimento* 3 (1929): pp.696-704.

132

Hales, E. E. Y. *Mazzini and the Secret Societies*. New York: P. J. Kenedy, 1954.

Halevy, Elie. *History of the English People in the Nineteenth Century*, 9 vols. London, 1909.

The Growth of Philosophical Radicalism. Translated by M. Morris, London: 1928.

Hammen, Oscar V. *The Red '48ers*. New York: Charles Scribners Sons, 1969.

Hammond, J. L. and Barbara, *James Stansfeld: a Victorian Champion of Sex Equality*. London, 1932.

Harrison, Royden. *Before the Socialists*. London: Routledge and Keagan Paul, 1961.

Hayes, Carlton J. *The Historical Evolution of Modern Nationalism*. New York: Russell and Russell, 1968.

Hearder, H. "The Making of the Roman Republic.," *History* 60 (1970): pp. 169-184.

Himmelfarb, Gertrude. *Victorian Minds*. New York: Alfred A. Knopf, 1968.

___ *On Liberty and Liberalism;* The case of John Stuart Mill. New York: Alfred A. Knopf, 1974.

___ *The Idea of Poverty: England in the Early Industrial Age*. New York: Alfred A. Knopf, 1984.

Hinkley, Edyth. *Mazzini*. Port Washington: Kennekat Press, 1924.

Hoenig, F. W. "Letters of Mazzini to W. J. Linton," *Journal of Modern History*, 5 (1933): pp. 58-60.

Holmes, Colin., ed. *Immigrants and Minorities in British Society*. New York: Macmillan, 1978.

Houghton, W. E. The *Victorian Frame of Mind*: 1830-1870.

____ ed. *The Wellesley Index to Victorian Periodicals, 2 vols.* Toronto University Press, 1966, 1972.

Hovell, Mark, *The Chartist Movement*. Edited by T. F. Tout. New York: Augustus M. Kelley, 1967.

Kaplan, Fred. *Thomas Carlyle*. Ithaca: Cornell University Press, 1983.

Kadish, Alon. *Apostle Arnold, the Life and Death of Arnold Toynbee 1852-1883*. Duke University Press, 1986.

King, Bolton. *The Life of Joseph Mazzini*. London: J. M. Dent, 1902.

Levi, A. *Mazzini*. Turin: Einuardi, 1955.

Lehman, B. H. *Carlyle's Theory of the Hero*. New York: A.M.S. Press, 1966.

Lichtheim, George. *A Short History of Socialism*. New York: Praeger Publishers, 1971.

Limentani, U. *L'attivita letteraria di Giuseppe Mazzini*. Turin: Einuardi, 1950.

Lippencott, B. E. *Victorian Critics of Democracv*. New York: Octagon Books, 1964.

Lowith, Karl. *From Hegel to Nietzsche, the Revolution in Nineteenth Century Thought*. New York: Macmillan, 1964.

Luzio, A. *La Madre di Giuseppe Mazzini*. Turin: Bocca, 1920.

Mazzini Carbonaro. Turin: Bocca, 1920.

"Mazzini's Metamorphoses," *The Living Age*, October, 1921, p. 45.

Carlo Alberto e Mazzini. Turin: Bocca, 1923.

Lyttelton, Adrian. ed. *Italian Fascisms From Pareto to Gentile* New York: Harper and Row, 1975

Mack-Smith, Denis. *Victor Emmanuel, Cavour, and the Risorgimento*. London: Macmillan, 1971.

Maccoby, S. *English Radicalism, 1832-52*. London: Thomas Nelson, 1935.

English Radicalism, 1853-1886. London: Thomas Nelson, 1938.

Mario, Jesse White. *The Birth of Modern Italy*. London: 1909.

Mayer, Gustav. *Frederich Engels*. 2 vols. The Hague: Mouton and Co., 1934.

Migliori, F., ed. *Roma nel 1848-49*. Florence: La nuova Italia, 1968.

Manuel, Frank E. *The Prophets of Paris*. New York: Harper and Row, 1965.

Maseni, Pier Carlo. ed, *M. Bakunin: Ritratto dell' Italia borghese 1866-1871*. Bergamo, 1961.

Maximoff, G. P. *The Political Philosophy of Bakunin*. London: Macmillan, 1953.

McCloskey, H. G. *John Stuart Mill: A Critical Study*. London: Macmillan, 1971.

McCunn, John. *Six Radical Thinkers*. London: Arnold, 1907.

McKay, D. "Joseph Cowen e il Risorgimento." *Rassegna Storica del Risorgimento* 51 (1964): pp. 5-26.

Momigliano, Felice. "Mazzini e Carlyle," *Rassegna Italo-britannica*. 1 (1918): pp. 18-36.

Monaco, M. "L'Idea di nazione in Giuseppe Mazzini e in Pasquale Stanislao Mancini," *Rassegna Storica del Risorgimento* 24 (1972) pp. 216-236.

Morelli, Emilia. *Mazzini: quasi una biografia*. Rome: Istituto per la Storia del Risorgimento, 1985.

L'Inghilterra di Mazzini. Rome: Istituto per la Storia del Risorgimento, 1965.

Mazzini in Inghilterra. Florence: Felice Le Monnier, 1938.

Morgan, R. P. *German Social Democrats in the First International, 1864-72*. Cambridge: University Press, 1964.

Morley, John. *The Life of William Gladstone*. New York: Macmillan, 1932.

Neff, Emery E. *Carlyle and Mill*. New York: Columbia University Press, 1924.

Nettlau, Max. *Michael Bakunin*. Berlin, 1901. Bakunin et l'Internationale. Geneva, 1926.

Nevler, V. E. "Un altra lettera inedita di Mazzini a Herzen," *Bol. della Domus Mazziniana* 28 (1982): pp. 5-7.

Onnis, P. "Battaglie democratiche e Risorgimento n un carteggio inedito di Giuseppe Mazzini e George Jacob Holyoake," *Rasseqna Storica del Risorgimento* 2 (1935): pp. 212-219.

Oriani, A. *Fino a Dogali*. Bologna: 1923.

Packe, Michael. *The Life of John Stuart Mill*. London: Secker and Warburg, 1954.

____ *Orsini*. Boston: Little, Brown and Company, 1957.

136

Padover, Saul K. *Karl Marx, An Intimate Biography*. New York: Mentor Books, 1980.

Palm, Franklin J. *England and Napoleon III*. Durham: Duke University Press, 1948.

Pankhurst, Richard. *The Saint Simonians, Mill, and Carlyle*. London: Sidgwick and Jackson, 1957.

Parkes, Kineton. *The English Republic*. London, 1891. "William James Linton." Bookman's Journal and Print Collector, 8 July, 1921.

Partridge, Monica. "Alexander Herzen and the English Press," *Slavonic Review* 36 (1958): pp. 78-89.

Pennacchini, L. "Dopo la caduta della repubblica romana," *Rassegna Storia del Risorgimento* 22 (1935): pp. 161-173.

Perillo, G. "Instanze di rinnovameto sociale e risonanza dell' Internazionale a Genova avanti la Comune parigiana," *Movimento Operaio e Socialista* 11 (1965): pp. 81-126.

Peruta, Franco. *Scrittori Politici dell' Ottocento*. Milan: Ricardo Ricciardi, 1969.

Pivano, Livio. *Lamennais e Mazzini*. Turin: Einuardi, 1959.

____ "Mazzini Dittatore, 1849," *Nuova Antologia* 61 (1926): pp. 265-269.

Plummer, Alfred. *Bronterre: A Political Biography of Bronterre O'Brien 1804-1864*. Toronto: University Press, 1971.

Porter, Bernard. *The Refugee Question in mid-Victorian Politics*. Cambridge: Cambridge University Press, 1979.

Ravenna, L. *Il giornalismo mazziniano*. Florence: Le Monnier, 1939.

Ravindraathan, T. R. "Bakunin and the Italians." PhD. dissertation, Oxford University, 1978.

Rebora, Piero. "Lettere di Mazzini ad un Predicatore Gallese," *Nuovo Antologia* '18 (19") pp. 130-134.

Roberts, J. M. *The Mythology of the Secret Societies*. London: Oxford University Press, 1972.

Robertson, Priscilla. *Revolutions of 1848: A Social History*. New York: Harper and Row, 1969.

Rodelli, Luigi. La Repubblica Romana del 1849. Pisa: *Domus Mazziniana*. 1955.

Roe, W. G. *Lamennais and England*. London: Oxford University Press, 1966.

Romani, Giuseppe. ed., *Strenni dei Romanisti*. Rome: Staderini Editore, 1947.

Romano, A. *Storia del movimento socialista in Italia*. 3 vols. Milan: A. Giuffre, 1964.

Romeo, *Rosario. Cavour e il suo lavoro*. 2 vols. Bari: Editore Laterza, 1977.

Rose, Henry. *The New Political Economy*. London: J.M. Dent, 1911.

Rosa, L. de. "Un 'radical' inglese del secolo scorso, *Nuova rivista storica* 11 (1950) pp. 97-102.

Roselli, Nello. *Mazzini e Bakunin: dodici anni di movimento operai in Italia*. Turin: Einuardi, 1967.

Rosenberg, Philip. *The Seventh Hero*. New York: Macmillan, 1979.

Royle, Edward. *Victorian Infidels: The Origins of the British Secularist Movement, 1791-1866*. Manchester:Manchester University Press, 1974.

Rudman, Harry W. *Italian Nationalism and English Letters*. New York: Columbia University Press, 1940.

Saint-Armand, Imbert de. *France and Italy*. New York: Scribner's, 1899.

Salamone, A. William. *Italy in the Giolittian Era*. Philadelphia: University of Pennsylvania Press, 1960.

Salvemini, Gaetano. *Mazzini*. Stanford: Stanford University Press, 1957.

Salvatorelli, L. "Rapporti e contrasti fra Napoleon III e Mazzini nella politica europea fra il 1850 e il 1860," *Rassegna Storica del Risorgimento* 41 (1954): pp. 582-586.

The Risorgimento: Thought and Action. New York: Harper and Row, 1970.

Sanders. C. R. *Carlyle's Friendships and Other Studies*. Durham: Duke University press, 1977.

Saville, J. *Ernest Jones: Chartist*. London: Lawrence and Wishart Ltd., 1952.

Schoyen, A. R. *The Chartist Challenge*. London: Hunemann, 1958.

Scott, Ivan. *The Roman Question and the Powers*, 1848-1865. The Hague: Martinus Nijhoff, 1969.

Seigel, Jules Paul. *Thomas Carlyle: the Critical Heritage*. New York: Barnes and Noble, 1971.

Seton-Watson, R. W. *Britain in Europe, 1789-1914, a survey of Foreign Policy*. Cambridge: Cambridge University Press, 1937.

Sevi, N. "Intorno all'organizazione della 'Falange Sacra. *Rassegna Storica del Risorgimento* 41 (1954) pp. 360-397.

Shaw, C. "The impact of Mazzini upon the thought of the Republican Wing of the Chartist Movement in England,"*Bol. della Domus Mazziniana* 21 (1975): pp. 279-318.

Shine, H. *Carlyle and the Saint-Simonians* New York: Macmillan, 1930.

Silone, Ignazio. *The Living Thoughts of Mazzini*. London: Cassell and Co., 1946.

Simon, W. M. *European Positivism in the Nineteenth Century*. Ithaca: Cornell University Press, 1963.

Smith, F. B. *Radical Artisan: William James Linton*. Manchester:University Press, 1973.

"Espionage in the British Post Office, 1844." *Historical Studies* 54 (1970): pp. 128-143.

Southgate, Donald *The Most English Minister -- the polices and politics of Palmerston*. London: Macmillan, 1966.

Stephen, Leslie and Lee, Sidney., eds. *The Dictionary of National Biography*. 22 vols. London, 1921-1922.

Talmon, J. L. Political Messianism: *The Romantic Phase*. New York: Harper and Row, 1960.

Taylor, A. J. P. "European Mediation and the Agreement of Villafranca." *English Historical Review* 48 (1933): pp. 59-71.

___ *The Italian Problem in European Diplomacy*, 1847-1849. Manchester: Manchester University Press, 1934.

Thayer, William R. *The Dawn of Italian Independence: Italy from the Congress of Vienna, 1814 to the Fall of Venice, 1849.*, vols. New York: Houghton Mifflin Co., 1893.

Thomas, Paul. *Karl Marx and the Anarchists*. London: Routledge and Kegan Paul, 1980.

Tramarollo, G. "Un modernista mazziniano, Giovanni Pioli, ed il discorso di J. Toynbee alla scuola mazziniana di Londra," *Bol. Domus Mazziniana* 28 (1982) pp. 9-23.

Trevelyan, George Macaulay. *Garibaldi's Defense of the Roman Republic.* London: Macmillan, 1907. (Manin and the Venetian Republic of 1848. London: Macmillan, 1924.)

Treves, Renato. *La dottrina sansimoniana nel pensiero italiano.* Turin: Istituto giuridico dell' Universita di Torino, 1931.

Tsuzuki, Chushichi. *H. M. Hyndman and British Socialism.* London: Oxford University Press, 1961.

Urban, Miriam B. *British Opinion and Policy on the Unification of Italy, 1856-1861.* Scottdale: Mennonite Press, 1938.

Ward, A. W., Prothero, G. W., and Leathers, S., eds. *The Cambridge Modern History.* 13 vols. Cambridge: University Press, 1934.

Ward, J. T. *Sir James Graham.* New York: Macmillan, 1967.

Webb, R. K. *Modern England: From the Eighteenth Century to the Present.* New York: Dodd Mead, 1972.

Weisser, Henry. *British Working-Class Movements and Europe.* Manchester: Manchester University Press, 1975.

Wicks, Margaret. *The Italian Exiles of London 1816-1848.* London: J. M. Dent, 1937.

Wiener, Joel H. *Radicalism and Freethought in Nineteenth Century Britain: The Life of Richard Carlile.* Westport: Greenwood Press, 1983.

War of the Unstamped. Ithaca: Cornel University Press, 1965.

Index

Wagner, Monique

FROM GAUL TO DE GAULLE
An Outline of French Civilization

New York, Bern, Frankfurt/M., Paris, 1989. XVI, 326 pp., 49 ill.
American University Studies: Series 9, History. Vol. 43
ISBN 0-8204-0729-1   hardback US $ 45.00/sFr. 67.50

Recommended prices – alterations reserved

This text is a concise publication on France, the land, its people and its great contribution to world culture. It contains a chronological account of the most important events which have shaped France and the French society in the course of centuries and a compact overview of the country's arts and letters. It is a guide to places of interest, historic sites, famous monuments and art treasures and provides essential information for all those interested in France. It is suitable also for use as a college manual of French Civilization, a "companion to French studies" and a "travel companion" to sophisticated visitors of France.

Contents: A Survey of French Civilization: geography, history, arts, literature, society, institutions, including a list of "things to see" and followed by a list of "things to remember", an Appendix with excerpts from selected literary masterpieces and a brief Chronology.

". . . That Professor Wagner (has) succeded, without oversimplifying complex issues or ignoring subtle distinctions in such a broad arena, is a tribute to her ability as a perceptive scholar and a skillful writer." (Martin M. Herman, Wayne State University)

"This accessible and attractive text ties together accurately and concisely historic and cultural developments and enlightens them in fascinating detail . . . its pace is quick enough to read almost as a novel." (Brian Morton, The University of Michigan)

". . . Both timely and unique in its kind . . . It will be very useful to the profession." (Richard Vernier, Wayne State University)

PETER LANG PUBLISHING, INC.
62 West 45th Street
USA – New York, NY 10036